ATTRACTION & HOSTILITY

THE ATHERTON PRESS
BEHAVIORAL SCIENCE SERIES

William E. Henry, General Editor
The University of Chicago

Published simultaneously in Great Britain
by Prentice-Hall International, London

ATTRACTION & HOSTILITY

An Experimental Analysis

of Interpersonal and

Self-Evaluation

ALBERT PEPITONE

ATHERTON PRESS

A Division of Prentice-Hall, Inc.

70 Fifth Avenue, New York, N.Y., 10011

ATTRACTION & HOSTILITY
Albert Pepitone

Preface

Social psychology's interest in attraction and hostility can be traced back to the formative years of the discipline, when sociologically oriented scholars focused their attention on gregariousness, crowd violence, and other topics reflecting man's liking and disliking of other people. The concern continues on the present scene, where matters like aggression, intergroup hostility, group cohesiveness, self-evaluation, and the need for affiliation are ubiquitous in the research literature. For all its significance, however, there is no organized body of knowledge which can even pretend to cover the field of attraction and hostility. This partly owes to the enormous range and kind of human behavior encompassed by these terms. So great is the diversity of data that it is difficult to imagine a comprehensive taxonomy, much less an integrated theoretical structure. In the face of this situation, I have become increasingly convinced that, rather than continue to formulate and deal with general concepts and models which vaguely explain almost everything under the sun, social psychology should somehow delimit and dimensionalize these phenomena. Theories developed to handle such relatively circumscribed data would be able to make a more detailed accounting of them. In addition, such low-level theories would be more easily modified and displaced than more abstract constructions, which are notoriously imperturbable.

In keeping with this idea, this book focuses on what appears to be a common denominator of a good many attraction and hostility measures—interpersonal and self-evaluation. No doubt even this is too general a domain to be handled by any single theory: What determines the evaluation of another's ability may differ from what determines the evaluation of his love of country. The risk here of an overgeneralization is, however, inordinately less than in the case in which the theory, by not specifying any universe of discourse at all, impliedly handles the whole of attraction and hostility and then some.

The current diffuseness of knowledge about attraction and hostility phenomena also requires a simplification of research methodology. Until our knowledge and technology are such that we can gain control over all relevant variables in single, decisive experiments, it appears necessary to test hypotheses by whole programs of relatively simple studies arranged in rational sequence. In principle, each successive study adds the information which was uncontrolled or found lacking in the preceding study. Of course, the step-by-step, programmed approach does not imply uniform designs in which identical operational measures are employed in every study. Indeed, it is probably the case that a variety of experimental arrangements and operational measures can strengthen and enrich a theory faster than a program completely homogeneous in these respects. At any event, the measures of interpersonal and self-evaluation used in the program of studies reported in this book are diversified. They include various quantitative ratings and "open-ended" verbal expressions and communications, as well as choice behavior and button-pressing. There was no philosophical position such as "phenomenology" or "neobehaviorism" which governed the selection of such measures; we used those which were feasible and appropriate in the circumstances.

Despite the eminent plausibility of the research strategy we have pursued, there is no thought that the hypotheses tested are, in their present form, absolutely true and immortal. In contemporary social psychology, it is a fact of life that more than one theoretical interpretation can almost always be offered for any given experiment. What we have tried to do is to make certain interpretations, consistent throughout a body of interrelated experiments, more probable than others. The observation that it remains for future studies to pin conclusions down more precisely is not a hedge but an appraisal that, at the present time, we are at least as much engaged in isolating and sharpening variables as in establishing invariant laws.

The central thesis that interpersonal and self-evaluations are in part determined by a cognitive-validation process seems like an intuitively obvious proposition. After all, would it make sense to postulate a need to distort social and self-evaluations? Yet, it is equally obvious that many interpersonal and self-evaluations fly in the teeth of rationality as defined by generally accepted criteria. Then too, several findings derived from the assumption of a cognitive-validation need—for example, that under certain conditions, more severe ethical violations lead to *less* self-defensiveness, self-depreciating persons are liked, and individuals with high self-esteem attribute more of their unfavorable characteristics to others than those with low self-esteem do—are not readily classified as banal, common-sense observations. By exposing the workings of a validation mechanism in interpersonal relations and self-attitudes, we are not implying that man is rational in the sense of a philosophical typology or grand scheme about human nature. The point is that whether and to what extent any individual is observed to validate his evaluations of others or of himself depends upon the presence and strength of other determinants of such evaluations besides validation and upon the validity criterion used—which, of course, may not be the same as the generally accepted one. The book is essentially a detailed analysis of the major forces underlying various interpersonal and self-evaluations.

It is my pleasure to acknowledge the considerable help I have received in carrying out the research reported in the book and in the preparation of the book itself. First, warm thanks are owed to my present and former graduate and undergraduate assistants, whose contributions include helping design experiments, conducting the studies, and analyzing the data: Frances Berger, Stanley Einstein, Ronald Feldman, David Gray, Allen Harris, Stephen Jones, Dr. Robert Kleiner, Dr. Donald Lauer, Dr. W. H. Wallace, and Dr. Abe Wolf.

I have profited from the criticisms and suggestions of several colleagues in social psychology who read early drafts of the manuscript. Especially helpful and constructive were Professors Theodore Newcomb, John Thibaut, and Harold Kelley. I have also gained much from conversations with European confreres about some of the ideas directly or indirectly dealt with by the book: Dr. Claude Faucheux and Dr. Jacques Ardoino of France, the late Professor Andrzey Malewski of Poland, and Dr. Guido Cohen of the Netherlands. Professor Herman Hutte (University of Groningen, Netherlands) to whose department I was attached as a Fulbright research professor, deserves thanks for the research facilities he generously made available to me. I should also thank my colleagues in the Department of Psychology at the University of Pennsylvania, who have created a climate for research which would be hard to match anywhere. And, like most social psychologists in the United States, I am enormously grateful for the support and encouragement of Luigi Petrullo of the Group Psychology Branch of the Office of Naval Research (ONR). Almost all of the studies reported in this book were done under contract with ONR, and it is not an exaggeration to say that without this support the work would never have been done. Finally, I want to acknowledge with profound gratitude the many contributions of my wife, Dr. Emmy Pepitone. Apart from providing sound critical advice and constant encouragement, she conducted one of the experiments, helped with the data analysis of many studies, and worked with me at every stage in the preparation of the book.

Philadelphia
March 1964

Contents

xi

List of Tables

xv

I Theoretical Considerations

INTRODUCTION TO PART I

Attraction and hostility in a bewildering variety of forms seem to characterize every kind of human relationship. A man denounces his neighbor, a worker praises his foreman, a diplomat writes a negative evaluation of his assigned country, a husband and wife call each other vile names, union and management leaders excoriate the mediator, a boy and girl declare their mutual love, and an angry crowd threatens an integration leader.

It is generally agreed that such phenomena should be explained and made predictable by the behavioral sciences, but it is also inescapably clear that no theories, at present, can do the job. Perhaps one reason for the slow progress in the accumulation of precise knowledge is that theories have become so overgeneralized that they cannot easily be rejected. In attempting

3

to encompass a maximum range and diversity of data, concepts have had to be defined at rarefied levels of abstraction. As a result, flatly contradictory data are hard to come by. For instance, a cumulative look at the behavioral-science literature might well lead one to suppose that war, suicide, marital discord, juvenile delinquency, crowd hysteria, and many other phenomena are the direct consequences of "frustration." Although manifestly an oversimplified explanation, the concept of frustration has persisted tenaciously. Indeed, because of its apparent generality, the concept exudes an aura of scientific power and invincibility which has made it preferred to less abstract interpretations.

Furthermore, even though most prevailing theories are too general, their applications do not consistently range over the same domain of data. This means that rigorous comparisons as to their adequacy in handling given phenomena become difficult. For example, although intergroup and interpersonal hostility have not been neglected altogether, the group-dynamics approach to social psychology has been more concerned with the causes and consequences of interpersonal attraction. Individually oriented social psychology, on the other hand, has emphasized the study of aggression virtually to the exclusion of the attraction sector. The question arises—are there laws of aggression which are different from laws of interpersonal attraction, or can a single conceptualization cover both areas? To outline an answer to this question and to formulate the problem with which our experimental studies in Part II will be concerned, it will be useful to examine in some detail how the data of attraction and hostility have been conceptualized and explained by the major systematic approaches.

Chapter I examines the interpretations of group cohesiveness and individual aggression which, at least implicitly, are based upon highly general need-satisfaction or need-frustration models. Also considered within the satisfaction-frustration framework are interpretations of attraction and hostility data in terms of specific motivations, such as the need for status and security. In Chapter 2, several cognitive-consistency models which are relevant to attraction and hostility, including balance, congruity, and dissonance models, are described and evaluated in detail.

Finally, Chapter 3 analyzes a large variety of social behaviors which have been interpreted in terms of a specific cognitive motive or mechanism.

This survey of background theory strongly suggests that much of what lies in the vast and sprawling area of attraction and hostility can be interpreted as the reflection of a need in the individual to maintain a valid cognitive structure with respect to the valuation of himself and others. The experiments which form Part II of this book are devoted to testing the role and ramifications of this "cognitive-validation" need in a variety of attraction- and hostility-generating situations.

1 Need-Satisfaction and -Frustration Models

Of all the systematic approaches to social psychology, group psychology has concerned itself most directly with the data of interpersonal attraction. This approach conceptualizes attraction in terms of group cohesiveness. The *esprit* of military units, the morale of work groups, the level of community integration, the solidarity of the political left or right, the tight code of the underworld mob—these are all summarized by the term cohesiveness. Appropriate to this focus on group phenomena is the conceptual definition of cohesiveness which, according to Cartwright and Zander (1960), is "the resultant of all the forces acting on all the members to belong to the group" (p. 74). Although such a quantity exists only when a group exists, it is, as the definition implies, ultimately decomposable into the attractions which individuals have for the group. Indeed, the operational measures of cohesiveness most frequently used in research are based directly on *individual* acts and attitudes. A common index of cohesiveness is, for example, the frequency of "sociometric" choices—choices of friends or work partners made by individual group members among other group members or persons outside the group.

Although research applications of group cohesiveness have not dealt explicitly with the attraction of the individual for himself, such an aspect is implicit. If the individual is attracted to the group, it is not unreasonable to assume that, as a group member, some of the attraction is to himself. Presumably, to some extent, the conditions which affect the cohesiveness of the group affect the attitudes of the individual members toward themselves.

According to the group-dynamics conceptualization, the explanation of attraction is based both upon the needs of the individual and the characteristics of the group. Thus, if any motivation of an individual group member is held constant, his attraction to the group would theoretically vary with the amount of need satisfaction which the group can directly or indirectly mediate. The stronger the need which the group can satisfy, the greater the attraction. It has been customary to differentiate the various sources of need satisfaction provided by the group. The following classification is typical: Individuals are attracted to groups (or resist leaving them) because of the satisfactions derived from personal affiliation as such, because of the prestige gained through membership, because of the satisfactions provided by the group's achievement of its goals, or even more generally, because of the instrumental capacity of the group to mediate various social and nonsocial goals.

The need-satisfaction theory of cohesiveness has been stated at an extremely high level of generality and, thus, has the potential of great integrating power. From an empirical point of view, however, it is surely not known whether all social and nonsocial needs increase interpersonal attraction when satisfied by the group. Moreover, nothing in the formula predicts the particular kinds of behaviors and conditions which are need-satisfying or the particular behaviors which reflect cohesiveness. As most often stated, the specific forms of attraction actually measured—for example, sociometric choices—are conceived to be automatic reactions following need satisfaction; they play no special role in bringing about the satisfaction and are not any more predictable than other reflectors of cohesiveness. It would seem that, for understanding the dynamics of cohesiveness and for making detailed predictions, the need-satisfaction model is far too abstract and far too much in advance of available empirical information.

DRIVE FRUSTRATION AND INDIVIDUAL HOSTILITY

Quite possibly because of psychoanalytic influence, individual psychology has concentrated more on the phenomena of interpersonal hostility. Most of the experimental work has been concerned with various overt aggressive behaviors, including wholly verbal forms, as well as various physical actions and gestures.

The major conceptualization in the area of hostility has clearly been the frustration-aggression hypothesis (Dollard, Doob, Miller, Mowrer, & Sears, 1939). Indeed, the thinking about hostility has been all but dominated by this formulation. The basic statement of the hypothesis is simple: Frustration is a condition or event which prevents the occurrence of a goal-directed act. Frustration results in an instigation to aggression, and, if there is no inhibition to prevent it, the instigation results in an overt aggressive response. Conceptually, the goal of aggression is to injure the party at whom it is directed. When this goal has been achieved, the instigation to aggression is reduced. The greater the drive the response to which is frustrated, the greater the tendency toward aggression. Hostility toward the self can be understood either as an extreme, 180-degree displacement when the aggressive response toward the frustrator is inhibited or as a direct response to oneself as the frustrator.

Like the need-satisfaction theory of attraction, the frustration-aggression hypothesis is extraordinarily general. In the way it was originally stated, no distinctions whatever were demanded as to the nature of the interference or the nature of the drive the satisfaction of which is interfered with. A large variety of "blocks" have been used in research bearing on frustration-aggression; they include delays in obtaining rewards, motivational conflicts which prevent gratification, economic depression, failure to complete a task or to complete it successfully, being insulted, being kept up all night, and so on. However, existing experimental evidence is not sufficiently refined to show that it is the blocking characteristic as such which is responsible for the aggression. Moreover, there is more than a casual indication that some blocks do not produce any aggression at all or do so only under special conditions. According to everyday observation, at least, a physical obstruction or intellectual problem which blocks the progress of an individual often appears to produce a "re-organization," whereby the individual abandons his original goal and tries some other solution or tries to circumvent the barrier without palpable aggression. In animal studies, the partial-reinforcement technique, in which the reward is delivered on fewer than 100 per cent of the trials, can be interpreted as a frustration relative to the situation of 100 per cent reinforcement. Yet the consequences of such frustration, which include strengthened response tendencies and greater persistence under conditions of no reward, do not resemble anything like hostility.

Cognitive factors have been tied to the frustration model at a number of points. In the original formulation, for example, it was assumed that, as a goal response, aggression was directed toward injuring the source of the frustration. Presumably, a cognitive process is involved here in the location of the source of frustration. Cognition also plays a role in determining the amount of aggression. Pastore (1952) administered a question-naire containing a number of hypothetical frustrations which the subjects were to assume happened to them. In one experi-mental condition, the frustrations were described as "arbitrary" ("You're waiting on the right corner for a bus, and the driver intentionally passes you by"), whereas in a comparison condition, the same frustrations were phrased in a nonarbitrary fashion

("You're waiting on the right corner for the bus, when you notice that it is the Special on its way to the garage"). Significantly stronger aggressive reactions were found when the frustration was arbitrary. Of course, the nonarbitrary frustration evoked some aggressive responses, so it cannot be said that arbitrariness is a necessary condition for aggression. Indeed, the conceptual status of the arbitrariness variable is not altogether clear. It has been argued (Rothaus & Worchel, 1960) that it is not arbitrariness which increases the aggression; rather, nonarbitrariness inhibits the expression of aggression. In support of this thesis, these investigators show that "projected" aggressive responses—estimates by the subject of how others would react to the kind of hypothetical frustrations in the questionnaire study discussed above (Pastore, 1952)—were more frequent under nonarbitrary or "reasonable" conditions than were the subject's own aggressive responses. It may indeed be correct to assume that the subject is less inhibited when he responds projectively through someone else. But it is possible that subjects tend to think that others will perceive the situations as being less reasonable than they do and are therefore more likely to be aggressive. Arbitrariness as a determinant of aggression, in other words, cannot be unequivocally ruled out.

It has also been suggested that arbitrary frustration is essentially *unexpected* frustration. The disconfirmation of an expectation may be considered an additional frustration which leads to more aggression than would occur in a situation where frustration is expected (Berkowitz, 1962). This line of theoretical thinking is reflected in the interpretation of experimental results which show "contrast effects" in interpersonal evaluations (Berkowitz, 1960a, 1960b). Thus, when the subject's expectation of receiving friendly communications from other subjects is contradicted by the receipt of critical and hostile notes, the subject's evaluations of the other subjects are more negative than if the unfriendly behavior had been expected. This result would indeed seem to support the contention that frustrated expectations increase aggressiveness. But the same experiments show a symmetrical process at work. Subjects who expected unfriendly communications but actually received friendly communications evaluated their partners more positively than subjects who expected friendly behavior. Thus, if frustration is to apply to expectations, the concept must be expanded to predict increased liking as well as aggression, and a concept which predicts opposite behaviors without qualification would seem to have limited utility.

There is another aspect of the frustration interpretation of aggression which should be considered. As already mentioned, the occurrence of aggression, if it meets the criterion of a goal response, reduces the instigation to further aggression. This temporary decrease in aggressiveness is one form of what has been called the "catharsis effect." The unequivocal occurrence of catharsis has been difficult to demonstrate empirically, however. Typically, a reduction in aggressiveness following the expression of aggression can be explained by one or more alternative processes. In some experimental designs, one such alternative is provided by the frustration-aggression hypothesis itself: When the setup imposes a condition in which aggression is prevented, that is, frustrated, there should be increased subsequent aggressiveness. Now, when such a condition is compared with one in which aggression is freely permitted, no assumption about catharsis is needed to explain the existence of *relatively* less aggressiveness following its overt expression in the latter condition (Thibaut & Coules, 1952). Another alternative stressed by several writers in recent years (for example, Berkowitz, 1958) is that the expression of hostility sometimes constitutes a transgression which leads to guilt reactions. It may readily be supposed that the curtailment of aggressiveness represents one form of guilt reaction.

Formally speaking, in the drive-frustration model, the instigation to aggression is an automatic reaction. Just as a metabolic deficit leads to internal homeostatic responses which restore the equilibrium level or "steady state," frustration sets off aggressive responses which reduce the aggressive impulse. Unspecified, however, is the way in which injury of some kind, inflicted on an instigator, accomplishes this reduction. Such lack of specificity is especially troublesome since the aggression does not necessarily remove the frustration. In addition, the nature of the "block" requires analysis, as do the motivations that are blocked. Finally, more attention should be focused on the question: What *is* aggression? The formal definition of aggression—behavior which has injury as its aim—is notoriously question-begging and difficult to measure.

SOCIAL MOTIVES AS DETERMINANTS OF ATTRACTION

The foregoing analysis shows that the theoretical approaches to attraction and hostility by group and individual psychology are essentially based on a highly general model of need satisfaction or need frustration. For making detailed and precise predictions, however, a number of questions have to be answered: Which needs produce attractiveness when satisfied and hostility when frustrated? What particular conditions and behaviors are satisfying or frustrating? How are given forms of attraction and aggression produced when there is satisfaction or frustration of given motivations? Which specific acts and attitudes in the field of attraction and hostility are handled by the model, and which are not?

Accordingly, rather than employing the concepts of need or drive in general, some theorists have focused on more specific social motivations for explaining attraction and hostility. Research dealing with the need for affiliation and the need for achievement has been a step in the direction of greater specificity.

French (1956), for example, showed that the choice of partners for a given task depends upon the relevance of the task to one or both of these motivations. In order to arouse affiliative needs, Air Force trainees were requested to make friendship ratings of each other. Similarly, to arouse achievement motivation, subjects were told that a test of concept formation would be taken. Measures of the relative strength of the two needs thus aroused in the individual subjects were obtained by counting the number of achievement- and affiliation-relevant responses to projective-type questionnaire items. Next, work groups were made up by the experimenter so as to include three subjects who had chosen each other as friends and one who was not a friend of any of the others. The groups were then engaged in a card-sorting task, and it was arranged that only the nonfriend in each group obtained the one correct solution. Following this announcement, the experimenter explained that the subjects would work on the next task in pairs and requested each subject to write down the name of another member of the work group with whom he would like to work. The choices of partners made by the two major categories of subjects, high-achievement scorers and high-affiliation scorers, confirm a motivational-relevance hypothesis: High-achievement–oriented subjects tend to choose the successful (nonfriend) partner with greater frequency than do the high-affiliation–oriented subjects, whereas the latter choose a friend more often. But although this study shows that partner choice is based on the potential instrumental value of the partner for satisfying whichever need—affiliation or achievement—is regnant for the given individual, more information is needed concerning the conditions of motivational arousal and satisfaction.

Some theoretical questions about these social motivations may also be raised at this point. Although a more specific concept than need satisfaction, the so-called affiliation motive is circular. It begs the question as to the underlying dynamics of attraction. To break this circularity, we need to know what conditions arouse the affiliation drive, what people the individuals so motivated tend to associate with, and what particular conditions and behaviors satisfy such a motivation. As for the achievement need, it has been conceived as a highly individualistic drive, rooted in the individual's independence training as a child, and the very antithesis of social motives like affiliation. Such a conception seems to ignore a fundamental point, however. Aspiration and ambition with respect to most task and career goals can only be understood in relation to some standard which is social in nature. Moreover, as shown in the experiment just discussed, achievement motivation can be directly satisfied by the behavior of others and can thus move the individual toward the achievement which he desires. Achievement motivation, then, is more a social motivation than is acknowledged in most discussions of the concept. In any case, it too requires more detailed analysis in terms of the conditions which arouse it and satisfy it.

Moving toward a more specific and less circular conception, it could be proposed that attraction, as reflected in various affiliative attitudes and actions, is based on a need for dependency or security. Certainly, close attachment with primary groups can often be assumed to be based on the provision by the latter of support, love, feelings of belonging, guiltlessness, confidence, omnipotence, and so forth. But despite its apparent centrality to theories of attraction and hostility, experimental research on the determinants of security and insecurity is sparse. Arsenian (1943) demonstrated that children in a strange situation showed fewer signs of insecurity in the form of disorganized play, crying, temper, and the like when the mother or surrogate was present than when they were alone. Schachter (1959) and several investigators after him have presented some evidence that first-born and only children are more affiliation-prone in situations involving physical danger, such as the expectation of electric shock, than later-born subjects. One possible inference is that, because of the greater attention and love typically lavished on them, first and only children are more used to being dependent on others. It is also possible that the absence of siblings, at least for some period of development in early life, creates a relatively low threshold of anxiety and correspondingly strong dependency. More information is needed, of course, on the dynamics underlying this dependency or basic-insecurity theory of affiliation and attraction.

A second specific approach to achievement motivation, highly relevant to the subject of attraction, focuses on the concept of status. In Western civilization, at least, achievement of status or avoidance of loss in status—in terms of social, financial, educational, and other kinds of rank—are ubiquitous tendencies. Although many various definitions have been used to convey the meaning of status, there are two properties which most definitions have in common. The first is prestige—the position of a person on some implicit or explicit scale of what is socially valued. High prestige means that the individual is highly evaluated in some respect by one or more persons in his social environment who may be, to some degree, important to him. The second is power—the position of a person on some implicit or explicit scale which represents his ability to influence and control the social and physical environment.[1] The individual with power is one who can influence the behavior of other persons. It has been exceedingly difficult to separate these two components of status or to determine the direction and amount of their interdependence. Most dimensions of power—for example, political influence—also tend to correspond to a prestige scale. Indeed, prestige is one basis of power. The possession of power is a determinant of prestige, even if in a circumscribed area. It is also often the case that prestige and power, each based on an independent set of conditions, coincide in the same person. At any event, even though status motivation is not a unidimensional concept, it allows the specification of the basis of affiliation and achievement drives. Thus, status motivation is presumably aroused by conditions which affect the probability of achieving or losing prestige and/or power.

It is obvious that security and status motivations are closely interrelated. One person can move toward—be attracted to—another person or group in order to attain security or status or both. In striving to satisfy these motivations, the individual is often in conflict. To compete for status, he may run the risk of rejection and loss of security; to achieve maximum security, he may forfeit status achievement. When a person is devalued by another important person or group, there is the double threat of losing both security and status.

In their various interrelationships, it is clear that status and security are powerful determinants of attraction and hostility.

1. These, of course, are loose working definitions which are not intended to be complete. There are many useful distinctions which could be made within the prestige and power components of status. There are also several complex problems in determining the objective and subjective bases of power and prestige.

More particularly, research evidence shows that the attractive-ness of others varies with their capacity to satisfy security or status motivations which have been aroused in the individual. Conversely, if others threaten the status and security of the individual, their attractiveness tends to decrease.

For example, a competitive situation, in which the actions of one person to achieve a prestigious goal constitute adverse condi-tions for the others, tends to lower interpersonal attractiveness (Deutsch, 1949). In another study (Deutsch, 1959), it was shown that a high probability of success in a given group resulted in higher interpersonal attraction among its members. Of course, actual superior performance of one work group relative to an-other leads to greater mutual attraction within the group (Seashore, 1954).

The connection between social motivation and specific measures of attraction must be examined in greater detail. A hypothesis linking sociometric choices with both threatened loss and expected achievement in status was investigated in a con-trolled field experiment by Pepitone and Kleiner (1957). In this study, an attempt was made to create different quantities of status motivation and to observe the effect upon change in inter-personal attraction.

Pairs of teams, each consisting of four boys evenly matched in terms of their age and race, were engaged to play against each other in a series of competitive athletic games represented to them as an important and prestigious tournament. After a few closely fought contests in volleyball, touch football, and other camp sports, winning and losing teams in the preliminary phase of the tournament were announced, partly on the basis of faked scores. With some fanfare, a prize of high prestige value was awarded to each member of the winning teams. In this way, two levels of status were established and could serve as a basis for generating status-achievement and status-loss motivations. Teams which had lost the preliminary contest—*Low-Status* teams—were subjected to strong or weak expectations of winning the final contest, whereas teams which had won the preliminary phase—the *High-Status* teams—were exposed to strong or weak expectations of losing the final contest. Specifically, the status motivations were introduced by the experimenter announcing to each of the *High-Status* teams, with their corresponding *Low-Status* competitors present, either that they were likely to lose the final contest or that they were likely to maintain their winning position at the end of the tournament. Presumably, to the *Low-Status* team members present, the message implied either that they were likely to win the final contest or that they were likely to stay in their losing position. The effect upon change in interpersonal attraction was determined by a sociometric procedure undertaken at the very beginning of the preliminary series of games and again just before the end of the final contest. Attraction was measured by the number of companions for an overnight hike chosen or rejected from his own team by each individual team member. The average number of choices made after the experimental treatments was subtracted from the average number of "in-team" choices made initially. Thus, the extent to which the team members chose or rejected each other for this uncertain and possibly competitive event constituted a measure of the strength of interpersonal attraction.

The *High-Status* teams in which a weak expectation of a loss in status was induced showed a significantly greater increase in positive sociometric choices than the teams which were strongly threatened. Such a finding would appear to be in line with the general need-satisfaction model as it is applied to status motivation. However, some detailed assumptions are necessary. For one thing, the *High-Status* team members presumably see each other as the essential source of the threat or absence of threat to their individual and collective status. They hold themselves responsible for whatever likelihood there is of losing their status position as a team and as individuals. Thus, members of those teams which are told that they are in relatively little danger of losing status tend to regard themselves as highly capable of reducing social and other dangers, whereas members of teams which are told that they are probably going to lose consider themselves less capable. Sociometric choices for a somewhat uncertain future situation—one in which there might be

competition with other hiking groups, as well as physical dangers
—can be said to be a function of the perceived mutual capacity
to reduce social and physical threats. Although not a necessary
part of the theory, it is useful to assume that the choices operate
on the social environment—that is, that they instruct the camp
authorities on how to compose the hiking groups so that the
chooser's status in certain spheres (as well as his security) can be
maximized. According to this analysis, then, it is not status and
other social dangers directly which affect choices reflecting attraction, but rather the estimated capacity of individuals and
groups to cope with such potential social threats.

The differential expectations of winning the final tournament, experimentally communicated to the *Low-Status* teams,
did not affect the average change in frequency of their "in-team"
companion choices. However, the experimental variable was not
without effect. Team members who had weak expectations of
achieving victory in the tournament did, as would be expected,
play less vigorously and competitively than those whose expectation of winning was relatively strong. One plausible reason for
the lack of differential effect on the sociometric choices is that
being in a low-status position or having a history of losing games
tends to discourage the internal attribution of responsibility.
That is, members of the *Low-Status* teams did not see themselves
as exclusively responsible for the final outcome. Accordingly,
their choices of companions who could maximize social status
and security were directed less exclusively to each other.

This last point concerning the role of responsibility in
determining attraction obviously needs checking. It is also necessary to see whether an actual reduction in status threat produces
a corresponding increase in the attractiveness of the particular
individual who brings it about. Kleiner (1960) designed an experiment to confirm a more precise formulation of a social-motivational theory of attraction.

Groups consisting of two business-school subjects and a
confederate were given a test of problem-solving ability of a kind
which, they were led to believe, was of crucial importance for
success as an executive. Charts demonstrated that all the college

teams tested thus far had made the qualifying number of points. The experimenter mentioned that any team which did not reach the minimum standards would have to meet with personnel experts who would try to find out why it had failed. The implication was that its members would be humiliated and devalued in various ways. The test consisted of putting together six-piece picture puzzles in two sequential parts. After the first part, the teams were given either a high or low threat of failure on the basis of the points they had thus far earned. This initial status threat was given in the form of a probability statement. During the second part of the task, on the basis of prior knowledge concerning the correct sequence of fitting pieces, the confederate solved some of the puzzles which the two subjects could not solve. Thus, at the conclusion of the second part, the experimenter was able to announce to the teams that there had been a large reduction or a small reduction in the chances of failure. Sociometric measures dealing with the mutual evaluation of the team members as future work partners and as social companions confirmed the hypotheses that: 1) The greater the individual's responsibility for a reduction in status threat, the more attractive he is. (The subjects evaluated the confederate more positively than they evaluated each other.) 2) The greater the reduction in status threat brought about by an individual, the more attractive he is. (The confederate was evaluated more positively when he brought about a large reduction than when he caused a small reduction in threat of failure.) A further finding of interest for the quantitative elaboration of the theory was that reductions in threat which took place from a higher initial level of threat had a greater effect on the evaluation of the confederate, that is, resulted in higher attractiveness, than threat reductions which occurred from a lower initial level of threat.

The results of these experiments support the hypothesis that interpersonal attraction is proportional to the estimated capacity of individuals to maximize gains and minimize losses of status and security. The capacity factor depends on the extent to which the individuals are perceived to be responsible for each other's losses or gains in status and security, as well as on the amount of the losses or gains involved. There is also support for the idea that the particular responses reflecting attraction, such as sociometric choices, themselves function to bring about an optimal level of status and security. It may be noted that this theory of attraction differs from the simple, popular conception in which social and physical threats directly increase the solidarity and cohesiveness of groups. Indeed, disintegration and loss of attraction may result when there is insufficient capacity to minimize the threat.

SOCIAL MOTIVES AS DETERMINANTS OF HOSTILITY

Dissatisfaction with the cosmic scope of the frustration-aggression theory has, almost from the time it was first published, led a number of writers (Maslow, 1941; Rosenzweig, 1944, for example) to propose that a more restricted set of conditions than the blocking of a goal response be adopted for the explanation and prediction of hostility. In particular, actual or threatened loss of status, socially based self-esteem, and security have been cited as basic determinants of aggression. If the laboratory procedures actually employed to evoke aggressive actions and attitudes in subjects are considered, the relevant role of such specific social motivations seems clear. The procedure of McClelland and Apicella (1945) is typical. A student experimenter caused the subject to fail on a task. He then systematically insulted the subject's intelligence, integrity, and conscientiousness. In such circumstances, almost half of the countable verbal reactions were outright denunciations of the experimenter or diffuse expressions of anger. In the same laboratory tradition, Ax (1953), Feshbach (1955), and Pepitone and Reichling (1955) presumably threatened subjects with a loss of status by insulting their level of ability, motivation, physical attractiveness, maturity, and the like. Various forms of more or less strong hostility resulted from these operations.

Such status and security hypotheses of aggressive behavior appear to differ from the drive-frustration model only in point of specificity. Horwitz (1958), however, attempted to hold the degree of frustration constant while varying a specific social motivation. According to this investigator, hostility was a function of a reduction in the individual's "power" or adequacy in attaining goals. Operationally, "power" was defined by the weight or voting strength which the subjects were given in the making of a decision about whether to continue tasks that had been interrupted. In one condition, the leader (actually a confederate of the experimenter) had twice the weight of the subjects, whereas in a second experimental condition, the leader had only one quarter of the weight officially assigned to the subjects. In both conditions, subjects were led to believe that they had voted to repeat the first part of the task; in both conditions, however, the leader made the decision to continue the task. Thus, insofar as the subjects were prevented from making the "goal response" of repeating the first part of the task, the frustration was constant. In one condition, however, where the leader had only one-fourth of the legal authority, one could say that his decision illegitimately deprived the subjects of their power. In the other condition, where the leader had twice the legal weight of the subjects, their loss of power was legitimate. The leader had every right to go against the group decision. In terms of ratings reflecting the dislike of the leader and the attribution of unfavorable traits to him, the illegitimate loss of power produced significantly more hostility than the condition in which his decision to continue the task was made legitimately.

A theoretical formulation which would appear to represent the processes in such an experiment is as follows: Hostile tendencies are aroused in the individual when he is threatened with or actually suffers a loss in status or security. Overt hostile actions or attitudes are then directed toward the source of the threat in order to remove it. Descriptively, the directed behavior which is produced by a threatened or actual loss of status or security is defensive in function.

COGNITIVE FACTORS

The status- or security-defensive interpretation of aggression requires a role for cognitive factors just as the social-motivation interpretation of attraction does. If, for example, the individual is insulted by one whom he perceives as having the intention of being helpful, the individual does not consider the other's behavior an insult, and his aggressive response is weaker than in the case of a hostile intention (Pepitone & Sherberg, 1957). Further, the amount of aggressiveness, as well as its direction, is governed by the perceived justifiability or arbitrariness of the status threat and the degree of responsibility for launching it (Pepitone, 1958).

Although the influence of cognitive variables has been recognized in social-motivation interpretations of attraction and hostility, there is a serious question as to whether enough recognition has been given. Indeed, some experimental results can be reinterpreted to give the exclusive explanatory role to cognitive processes. Thus, in the Horwitz (1958) study, hostile attitudes toward the discussion leader were found to vary with his unwarranted usurpation of the group members' power. It is possible to suppose that the effective experimental variable was the unlawful act of the leader alone rather than its combination with the loss of power which the subjects sustained. It is conceivable that loss of power had nothing to do with the hostility and that the estimate that the leader was wrong could have been wholly responsible for the hostility directed toward him. More specifically, it might be conjectured that the subjects' negative evaluation of the discussion leader reflects a cognitive-validation process. In striving to maintain correct cognitions of the worth of others, the individual may have reevaluated the leader downward when he committed an unworthy act.

Such an interpretation can perhaps be applied to the results of many aggression studies where, in addition to the status and security threats, the "instigator" expresses extremely positive self-evaluations. If the latter are incorrect according to criteria which are considered reliable, the individual may reject them in forming a true valuation. The hostile attitudes, according to this view, are reflections of a validating process, as well as, or even instead of, reactions to the status or security threat.

A similar cognitive process may be involved to some extent in the so-called catharsis effect. For example, in an experiment dealing with the effect of cohesiveness on the ability of a pair of subjects to express aggression toward an instigator who had been insulting, it was shown that subjects in the experimental condition in which a larger amount of aggression was expressed also held subsequently a more positive evaluation of the instigator (Pepitone & Reichling, 1955). The catharsis effect is not the only interpretation for this. For example, the subject may have violated important internalized norms in expressing excessive hostility. If such norms are relevant to self-evaluation, violation of them could imply to the subject that his worth is lower than it was before the violation. If there is a need to maintain a valid self-evaluation, there should be a downward correction of the self-estimate following the violation. It is possible to interpret heightened attractiveness of the instigator as a reflection of such a self-correction.

With regard to attraction, the results of an experiment discussed earlier can also be reinterpreted in an exclusively cognitive light. It will be recalled that teams which were subjected to a relatively weak status threat in a competitive tournament showed a greater increment of positive, "in-team" sociometric choices than teams facing a relatively strong threat. It was proposed that, in the weak-threat condition, choices were more frequently directed toward each other by team members precisely because these players minimized a good deal of the status threat. They were "good bets" for future group activities in which there might be an element of competition. Instead of interpreting the choices as means of minimizing potential status or security threats, however, it is possible to consider the choices as reflecting re-evaluations which team members made of each other. Thus, in those teams where a greater reduction in threat had been brought about, the players considered each other more valuable persons in a certain realm of activity. They had worked harder and had apparently brought each other through a closely fought series of contests more skillfully. In short, their performance was more eminent than that of those team members who, according to the experimenter, had not done so well. This increment in the valuation of the successful team members was reflected in their being chosen more frequently. The important distinction here is between sociometric choices as re-evaluations demanded by the improved worth of the players and sociometric choices as instrumental responses toward removal of threats and facilitation of status achievement.

THE ARGUMENT IN SUMMARY

The vast array of data on attraction and hostility has frequently been interpreted in terms of highly general models. For example, the attraction of a group for its members—group cohesiveness—is said to be a function of the need satisfaction which the group is able to bring about. Similarly, the hostility of individuals toward other persons has most frequently been said to be a function of the frustration brought about by these persons. The need-satisfaction–attraction and the frustration-aggression formulations, although elegant in their simplicity and capable of tremendous integration of data, are not sufficiently detailed to provide a thorough understanding of or to predict specific forms of attraction and hostility. Required for these purposes is a knowledge of the kinds of needs and drives which are relevant to attraction and hostility, a knowledge of the behaviors and other conditions which constitute or lead to need satisfaction or drive frustration, and a knowledge of the process by which the condition of satisfaction or frustration comes to be reflected in the specifically measured forms of attraction and hostility. Because of such deficiencies, these general models can better be described as heuristic devices than as theories.

Conceptualizations of attraction and hostility have been proposed at lower levels of abstraction in terms of more specific needs. Thus, the sociometric attractiveness of persons is based upon their ability to reduce the threat of a status and/or security loss. Formulations about hostility also exist on this substantive level. Hostility is a function of the threat to an individual's status or is based on a loss of power suffered by the individual.

In the last analysis, however, much of the experimental work in support of a status or security explanation of attraction and hostility data can also be interpreted in terms of a cognitive process. In essence, at least some of the very attitudes and acts which have been based on status and security motives may be reflections of the individual's tendency to validate his cognitive structure concerning the valuation of himself and others. Before going into such a specific cognitive need in detail, however, it will be useful to examine, in the next chapter, some of the more general cognitive models which are relevant to the data of attraction and hostility.

REFERENCES

Arsenian, Jean M. "Young Children in an Insecure Situation," *Journal of Abnormal and Social Psychology*, XXXVIII (1943), 225–249.

Ax, Albert F. "The Physiological Differentiation Between Fear and Anger in Humans," *Psychosomatic Medicine*, XV (1953), 433–442.

Berkowitz, Leonard. "Repeated Frustrations and Expectations in Hostility Arousal," *Journal of Abnormal and Social Psychology*, LX (1960), 422–429. (a)

——— "Some Factors Affecting the Reduction of Overt Hostility," *Journal of Abnormal and Social Psychology*, LX (1960), 14–21. (b)

——— *Aggression: A Social Psychological Analysis*. New York: McGraw-Hill, 1962.

Cartwright, Dorwin, and Zander, Alvin. *Group Dynamics: Research and Theory*. Chicago: Row Peterson, 1960.

Deutsch, Morton. "The Effects of Cooperation and Competition Upon Group Process," *Human Relations*, II (1949), 129–152.

——— "Some Factors Affecting Membership Motivation and Achievement Motivation," *Human Relations*, XII (1959), 81–95.

Dollard, John, Doob, L., Miller, N., Mowrer, O., and Sears, R. *Frustration and Aggression*. New Haven: Yale University Press, 1939.

Feshbach, Seymour. "The Drive-reducing Function of Fantasy and Behavior," *Journal of Abnormal and Social Psychology,* L (1955), 3–11.

French, Elizabeth G. "Motivation as a Variable in Work Partner Selection," *Journal of Abnormal and Social Psychology,* LIII (1956), 96–99.

Horwitz, Murray. "The Veridicality of Liking and Disliking," in Renato Tagiuri and Luigi Petrullo, eds., *Person Perception and Interpersonal Behavior.* Stanford, Calif.: Stanford University Press, 1958.

Kleiner, Robert J. "The Effects of Threat Reduction Upon Interpersonal Attractiveness," *Journal of Personality,* XXVIII (1960), 145–155.

McClelland, David C., and Apicella, F. S. "A Functional Classification of Verbal Reactions to Experimentally Induced Failure," *Journal of Abnormal and Social Psychology,* XL (1945), 376–390.

Maslow, A. H. "Deprivation, Threat and Frustration," *Psychological Review,* XLVIII (1941), 364–366.

Pastore, Nicholas. "The Role of Arbitrariness in the Frustration-Aggression Hypothesis," *Journal of Abnormal and Social Psychology,* XLVII (1952), 728–731.

Pepitone, Albert. "Attributions of Causality, Social Attitudes, and Cognitive Matching Processes," in Renato Tagiuri and Luigi Petrullo, eds., *Person Perception and Interpersonal Behavior.* Stanford, Calif.: Stanford University Press, 1958.

Pepitone, Albert, and Reichling, George. "Group Cohesiveness and the Expression of Hostility," *Human Relations,* VIII (1955), 327–337.

Pepitone, Albert, and Sherberg, Janet. "Cognitive Factors in Interpersonal Attraction," *Journal of Personality,* XXV (1957), 757–766.

Rosenzweig, Saul. "An Outline of Frustration Theory," in J. McV. Hunt, ed., *Personality and the Behavior Disorders.* New York: Ronald, 1944.

Rothaus, Paul, and Worchel, Philip. "The Inhibition of Aggression Under Non-Arbitrary Frustration," *Journal of Personality,* XXVIII (1960), 108–117.

Schachter, Stanley. *The Psychology of Affiliation.* Stanford, Calif.: Stanford University Press, 1959.

Seashore, Stanley. *Group Cohesiveness in the Industrial Work Group.* Ann Arbor, Mich.: Institute for Social Research, 1954.

Thibaut, John W., and Coules, John. "The Role of Communication in the Reduction of Interpersonal Hostility," *Journal of Abnormal and Social Psychology,* XLVII (1952), 770–777.

2 Cognitive-Consistency Models

In the past decade, there has been a prolific development of cognitive models for dealing with attraction and hostility. Behind this surge of theoretical thinking lies an interest in the phenomenological analysis of behavior—placing a close-up lens on human experience—as well as a dissatisfaction with the alleged neglect of intellective and rationalistic factors on the part of need-satisfaction models. Of course, cognitive and need-satisfaction approaches do not differ in every respect in which they are comparable. As already mentioned, cognitive variables play important auxiliary roles in the status- and security-threat interpretations of hostile and aggressive behavior. Furthermore, cognitive models essentially describe an equilibrium tendency which, in a formal sense, is no different from that underlying

28

the need-satisfaction models. What appears most to distinguish cognitive models is the emphases placed upon consistency and rationality as determinants of behavior in their own right and upon the idea of disequilibria among cognitions or elements of meaning. There are three highly general cognitive approaches to the phenomena of attraction and hostility: the balance model, the congruity model, and the dissonance model. To assess their contribution to the state of knowledge in this area, it is necessary to examine each of them in some detail.

THE BALANCE MODEL

In his highly original and influential book, Heider (1958) outlines a "common-sense" psychology of interpersonal relations to deal with such questions as how a person perceives and acts toward other persons and himself, how he expects others to perceive and act toward him, and how he reacts to the behavior of others. The concepts employed by common-sense psychology are found in the language with which such phenomena are commonly described. For example, the verbs "to give," "to take," "to receive," and "to keep" describe a certain class of actions in terms of who originates them and the direction in which objects are transferred from one person to another. Behavioral distinctions also emerge from linguistic connotations. The verb "to steal," for example, connotes actions which violate social norms. Such actions can be considered members of a class defined by the verb auxiliaries, "ought" and "ought not." In addition to language itself as a source of concepts, popular descriptions of interpersonal situations often reveal an implicit conceptual structure. Fables like "The Fox and the Crow" illustrate motivational concepts like *wanting* (the crow wants the cheese), structural concepts like *belonging* (the cheese belongs to the crow), and action concepts like *causing* (the fox causes the crow to open his beak).

The analysis of interpersonal relations in terms of such "common-sense" concepts appears to illuminate their causal dynamics. The apparent illumination, however, may owe to the absence of traditional theoretical approaches as serious competitors in the realm of commonplace behavior. It is widely held that explanations which can be verbalized by the untutored layman are *ipso facto* invalid or trivial. Although such a view certainly cannot be defended on logical grounds, it is true that naïve concepts are too dependent upon the astuteness of an individual analyst and upon linguistic apparatus and tradition. Clearly, concepts whose source is in the language are highly "culture-bound" and fickle. They are subject to change by an agency—the public—not especially concerned with building a body of scientific knowledge. Moreover, naïve concepts lack the formal attributes and quantitative dimensions that are necessary for scientific generalization. Because of these limitations, a more abstract theoretical conceptualization of interpersonal relations is necessary. The cognitive-balance hypothesis represents such a theoretical step.

The domain of the balance tendency is the individual's "cognitive field" in which objects such as other persons, the self, groups, ideas, and other cognizable entities are represented. Such objects tend to be organized into units. At the simplest level of structural organization, some objects are cognized as belonging together, whereas others are experienced as segregated. The determinants of such "unit formations" include similarity, proximity, ownership, causality, and other factors which Gestalt psychologists have identified as organizing factors in the perception of the physical world. For example, an act and the individual who caused it tend to be seen as a unit; objects which are owned and the individuals who own them tend to be seen as cognitive units. Of special relevance to social behavior are unit formations based on kinship, race, nationality, social class, age, and other criteria of grouping. Cognitive unit formations are defined not only by properties of the objects themselves, but by the relation of these common properties to the surrounding field. This observation about cognitive organization has implications for attraction and hostility. For example, some social relationships appear to be based on antipathy of the parties in the relationship toward outsiders. In the same way, coalitions seem to be affected by the relationship of the persons in the coalition to persons outside. If the third person is similar to the two persons in a coalition, the coalition tends to be weaker than if the third person is dissimilar.

In addition to structural relatedness or separateness, cognized objects are also characterized by dynamic properties. These are positive and negative values attached to the objects by the cognizer himself. These values correspond to his likes and dislikes of the objects or attitudes which he understands others to have toward the objects. In general, then, the cognitive field in which balance tendencies operate consists of unit formations based on "unit relations" and "liking relations" among the objects cognized therein.

Stated simply, the balance hypothesis asserts that there is a tendency for attitudes toward objects which are part of a unit formation to be uniform and for those objects toward which attitudes are uniform to become unit formations. A balanced state is one in which the unit formation and the attitudes toward the objects in the unit formation coexist harmoniously. If a balanced state does not exist for the person, he experiences a pressure to change either the unit formation, by way of cognitive restructuring or action, or the attitudes.

With respect to the dyadic relationship—which consists of the person whose cognitive field is being examined and another social or nonsocial object—a situation is balanced if the person likes an object with which he is in some way connected. Thus, if being similar to someone, or being associated with him in the same group, family, class, or club represents a unit structure in the person's cognitive field, the balance hypothesis predicts a tendency toward positive evaluation of the other person who is part of that unit formation. By the same token, familiarity, proximity, and other determinants of cognitive units should lead to positive attitudes toward those who are part of such units. Of course, the model predicts balance *tendencies*. Whether the situation actually becomes balanced for the individual in question depends upon what forces exist in opposition to the tendency.

The balance hypothesis may also be applied to the triadic

relationship, which involves the individual and two other social or nonsocial objects. In looking at triadic balances, considerable generality is gained if the liking relation is assumed to be functionally equivalent to a structural unit relation. Thus, for example, if P likes A and B likes A, then P should tend to like B. Both parties are connected with each other by virtue of their common attitude toward an object. Or, if P likes A and B, he should tend to think that A likes B and B likes A. Imbalance results when P likes A and B, but A does not like B, or when P likes A and P likes B, but B does not like A. Such a state of affairs should give rise to pressures toward change to bring the triad into balance.

The association between similarity and liking is seemingly ubiquitous in all human relationships. Similarity has been cited by laymen and sociologists as a determinant of interpersonal attraction such as that illustrated by marriage or the solidarity of the group. The reverse process whereby liking produces similarity has also been observed. In neither case, however, can it be unequivocally argued that balance pressure is responsible for the association. In citing balance pressure as the basis of the relation between similarity and liking, it must be assumed that the person has a positive attitude toward himself. It is this positive self-evaluation with which the evaluation of the other unit member is balanced. To confirm the balance hypothesis, it is necessary to show that the individual tends to evaluate a similar person negatively—or a dissimilar person positively[1]—when he has a negative evaluation of himself. In this connection, Lewin's (1948) penetrating analysis of self-hate in members of religious minorities, which is associated with hostility toward coreligionists, seems to be amenable to a balance interpretation.

In an experiment explicitly aimed at testing a balance hypothesis, Deutsch and Solomon (1959) predicted that an individual will positively value others whose evaluation of him is similar to his own self-evaluation and negatively evaluate those whose

1. It is necessary, of course, to distinguish the absence of a unit formation from the opposite of a unit formation. For instance, dissimilarity is the obverse of a unit formation; nonsimilarity is the absence of one.

evaluations of him are dissimilar to his own. If the individual evaluates some aspect of himself negatively, he should tend to like those who also regard this aspect negatively. On the other hand, he should dislike those who like that part of himself which he dislikes. But if the individual evaluates himself positively, he should tend to like those whose evaluation of him is also positive and dislike those whose evaluation of him is negative. To check these predictions, a high or low self-evaluation was experimentally induced in subjects by leading them to believe their performance on a task was superior or inferior relative to the group. After receiving their own scores and those of the other group members, subjects wrote spontaneous notes to each other concerning their opinions of each others' performances. The experimenter substituted negative or positive evaluations, distributing one to half of the subjects and the other to the other half. Using these notes as a basis, subjects were then instructed to form a "first impression" of the writer and indicate it on a number of rating scales. The results tended to bear out the predictions: Those subjects in whom a low self-evaluation was induced evaluated negative note writers more highly than they evaluated positive note writers. Those subjects in whom a positive self-evaluation had been induced evaluated positive note writers more highly than negative note writers. The statistical interaction shows that social evaluations tend to be consistent with self-evaluations. The balance effect was not the only one operating in the situation, however. Apparently, subjects tend to evaluate the positive note writer more favorably than the author of the negative notes.

In connection with the balance prediction that dissimilarity leads to hostile attitudes, it should be emphasized that dissimilarity can mediate various status and security threats for the individual. A "different" person may be expected to behave so as to cause the individual embarrassment or loss of prestige. Such threats could account for the negative evaluation in addition to, or even instead of, the sheer reaction to imbalance.

A further qualification of the similarity-balance prediction lies in the apparently contradictory observation, often cited in adages, that opposites attract each other. Whether any data of this kind represent true exceptions to the balance principle, however, appears to depend upon the level of analysis. Some positive relationships do exist between dissimilar persons, but the dissimilarity may reflect complementary roles or needs. On a deeper level, in other words, there *is* a common purpose. The potential interpretive difficulty here would be lessened if the existence of a unit formation was more clearly specified operationally.

Predictions of attraction are based on unit formations other than similarity in the strict sense of the term. There are, for instance, informal observations to the effect that spatial proximity, interaction, and familiarity determine attraction via balance tendencies. Yet there are obvious exceptions. Persons often dislike those with whom they are most familiar, closest, and with whom they interact most. These cases do not necessarily invalidate the balance hypothesis; they challenge its unqualified generality.

It was previously mentioned that a triad in which a person likes two others who dislike each other would be imbalanced and would be expected to lead to pressures toward bringing the triad into a balanced state. Festinger and Hutte (1954) present data relevant to this prediction. They induced a cognitive imbalance in half of their subjects by leading them to believe that the two persons in the group whom they liked the most did not like each other. The remaining members of the group were told that their two choices did like each other. At the end of the group discussion, the subjects were asked again to name two most attractive group members and to estimate, in the light of the discussion, how much these choices liked each other. It was found that subjects who presumably experienced a cognitive imbalance changed their choices more frequently and estimated that their two choices liked each other to a greater degree than did subjects under cognitive balance. But although the change in choices and the estimate of greater mutual attraction reflected greater balance, they could have been based on forces other than those produced by the state of cognitive imbalance. For instance, the individual whose friends do not like each other may be afraid of being accused of partiality or of being rejected by both for being traitorous or having divided loyalty. In other words, the restructuring could have been based on some form of social motivation rather than on the cognitive imbalance.

Apparent exceptions to balance occur in the triadic relation which describes a competitive situation. For instance, suppose that a person is motivated to attain some goal such as winning a prize and that the person has a classmate whom he knows is also bent on winning the prize. Under such circumstances, it is hardly likely that the person's evaluation of his classmate would become more positive. On the contrary, negative sentiments are far more predictable. Competition of this sort may not be a real exception to the balance hypothesis, however. For one thing, the goals of the competitors may not be similar. Although the prized object as such is identical, it might be argued that the goal has to do with who is to possess the prize. So, even though both like the prize, a unit formation is not necessarily implied. Moreover, if there is a unit formation based on ownership of a common object, it would conflict with another unit formation based on the person owning it. In cooperative relations, on the other hand, the individual's goal is not to possess the prize personally; it is the group as a whole which strives to attain the prize. Since the person and his teammate belong in the same unit formation, there is a tendency toward mutual positive evaluations.

The balance hypothesis in the triad encounters a difficulty of a most fundamental kind. A simple example will make the point. If a man is married to a woman he loves and his wife loves her mother, the balance hypothesis predicts that the man tends to love his mother-in-law. In a word, the triadic relationship is transitive: A likes B, B likes C, A likes C. But in real life, as well as in jokes, such a relationship is far from being inevitable. Again, a person typically loves the dog he owns but does not love the things the dog loves, such as sniffing at fire hydrants. It would seem necessary to assume that, for two or more social and self-evaluations to move into balance, they must exist on a unidimensional scale—be in the same realm of discourse. In the case of the dyad, there is a similar consideration to be made. When a person dislikes another who is similar to himself, it may not be the case that he dislikes himself. His evaluation of the other may be based on entirely different dimensions from the liking of the self.

The foregoing examples indicate that the balance tendency can probably be considered a restricted case of the tendency of interpersonal and self-attitudes and -evaluations to be mutually consistent. It may be that objects which are structurally connected in some way—that is, which are part of the same unit formation—are *expected* to have the same dynamic properties. But similar dynamic properties are not necessary consequences of membership in the same unit formation. Thus, an individual who evaluates himself positively does not always evaluate positively a person with whom he is connected in some way. The individual who thinks he has outstanding musical talent does not necessarily appreciate the language ability of his father with whom, according to a number of criteria, he is structurally connected. Attitudes toward language ability and musical talent may be, for the individual, entirely different realms of discourse. On the other hand, attitudes which lie along the same dimension and which theoretically tend to be consistent with each other surely do not have to be directed toward objects which are part of the same unit formation. An individual who thinks highly of his own musical talent may discover the genius of a very dissimilar stranger—one who is no way connected to him. It might well be the case, in short, that the tendency toward cognitive balance is based on a consistency need which can and does operate quite independently of unit formation. Something of this more general view of the balance hypothesis is implied when liking relations are regarded as functionally equivalent to structural relations. If A likes B, he tends to like many of the things B likes along the same or similar dimensions, regardless of B's presence in a unit formation with A.

Whatever the role of unit formation, the foregoing touches on the more basic question of what underlies the balance tendency. Why do people tend to like the things they own? Heider (1958) cautions against the assumption of a sheer automatic cognitive process. He does not believe that the balance model works because it is a mechanical system. Rather, the balance tendency is a manifestation of a more general organismic struggle toward perfection and harmony. The basis of balance lies in the structuring dynamics indigenous to the cognitive field. In this characterization, one can see the Gestalt concept of *prägnanz* or "simple structure" as a general determining factor. At another point, however, Heider (1958) suggests a somewhat more limited basis for the negative social evaluations resulting from a dissimilarity of beliefs. Differences in beliefs have implications for the person's grasp of the real world. Thus, if a person understands that there is a difference of belief on a given issue, his conception of the real world, reflected in his belief, may be threatened. Conceivably, it is this threat which somehow causes his negative evaluation of the person who disagrees with him.

Although, strictly speaking, his theory is not generated by a cognitive model, Newcomb (1953) has predicted a "strain toward symmetry" reflected by an individual's liking of another person who possesses similar beliefs. According to this view, the basis for the strain originates in the "reinforcement" history of the individual. Holding similar beliefs allows for optimal prediction of the other's behavior and communication with the other, and it reinforces the validity of the belief. Dissimilarity, on the other hand, frustrates or threatens the motives which are satisfied by these conditions. Such a line of argument presumably would assert that if dissimilarity of belief did not have this effect, there would not be any balance tendency.

THE CONGRUITY MODEL

Osgood and Tannenbaum (1955) have developed a cognitive model which is highly relevant to the interpretation of attraction and hostility data. The model applies to a more restricted area of interpersonal relations than does the cognitive-balance model. The main focus is on the situation where a more or less formal attempt is made to change the individual's attitudes toward issues, ideas, concepts, persons, and other social and nonsocial objects. In the paradigmatic research setting, there is an endorsement or nonendorsement of an object toward which the individual has an existing positive or negative attitude by a communicator (a "persuasive" source) who is also evaluated by the individual in a certain way. The attitudes toward object and source are typically measured on a 7-point scale (from +3 through 0 to −3) which reflects both the intensity and direction of these attitudes. The basic idea of the congruity model is simple. If the attitudes toward the object and toward the source who positively endorses the object are located at different positions along the scale, a state of disequilibrium is assumed to exist. Pressures toward making the attitudes congruent arise in an amount equal to the size of this discrepancy. Suppose, for example, that President Johnson urges citizens to support a candidate for the United States Senate. Suppose, further, that the particular citizen has an evaluation of the President represented by a +2 on the scale and that his existing attitude toward the senatorial candidate is a +1. Given these data, the congruity hypothesis would predict a change in the individual's evaluation of the President *and* of the candidate to the point on the scale where they are uniform. The amount of change, however, will not be the same for each attitude. It is a basic postulate of the congruity model that, the more extreme the attitude (either positive or negative), the greater the relative resistance it offers to congruity pressure. If, in the present example, the relative resistance to change is numerically equal to the degree of polarization of each attitude, two parts of the total pressure to change will be resisted by the attitude toward the President, whereas the attitude toward the candidate will resist one part of the total pressure to change. Accordingly, the evaluation of the President should drop the amount it is free to drop, namely, one-third of the unit distance to 1.67, while the evaluation of the senatorial candidate should change two-thirds of the distance to this position of equilibrium.

The congruity model also is capable of making predictions about attractions in more intimate dyadic relationships. Let us suppose the individual is considering prospects for a job as his research assistant and that a colleague whom he likes (+3) recommends a young man who, as far as the individual is concerned, has a record of being an indifferent performer (−2). In such a case, the congruity pressure is equal to 5, corresponding to the number of steps which either attitude would have to move in order to become congruent with the other. The predicted equilibrium point, however, again depends on the relative resistance offered by the attitudes. Because of its greater polarization, the evaluation of his colleague will be lowered two-fifths of the total discrepancy, while his evaluation of the recommended assistant will become more positive, moving three-fifths up the scale. The predicted position of congruency for the two attitudes is thus at +1. It is interesting to note that, because he endorsed a disliked candidate, the colleague comes to be liked less than if he had kept quiet.

As a result of congruity pressure, the individual can also come to like another person more than he did before. Thus, suppose the individual is very excited about a car (+3) which a colleague whom he does not particularly like (−2) claims is the finest piece of machinery on the road. In such an event, congruity pressure should cause the individual to look somewhat more favorably upon his colleague. Indeed, because of the less extreme attitude toward him, the colleague will become more attractive than the car will become unattractive. These examples illustrate the point that congruity pressure affects both attitudes, except where one of them is at the zero point, in which case it is this neutral attitude which does all of the changing.

So far, we have been discussing the case where the source communicates an endorsement of, or in some other way positively evaluates, a social or nonsocial object. The congruity model also applies to sources who reject or make negative assertions about objects. In this event, congruence occurs when attitudes are equal in strength but opposite in sign. When a disliked source denounces a person who is liked as much as the source is disliked, the attitudes are congruent for the individual. Specifically, if an individual hears his good friend (+3) harshly criticized by a person whom he tends to dislike (−1), congruency will occur for him if he lowers his evaluation of the friend two steps to +1 and his evaluation of the disliked person from −1 to −3. Again, of course, the prediction of how much of the two-unit distance each of these evaluations actually moves depends upon the relative resistances of the two evaluations.

In general, then, congruity pressure and consequent attitude change are predicted when there is a discrepancy between the individual's evaluation of some social or nonsocial object and his evaluation of a source who positively evaluates the object; or when the evaluations are the same, and the source negatively evaluates the object. But what is the basis of the movement toward congruence in such instances? The mere holding of different attitudes toward sources of communication and toward objects is not a sufficient condition for attitude change. What apparently is necessary is the "associative" or "disassociative" relation which the source creates between the individual's attitude toward the source and the object which the source endorses or disapproves of. Indeed, the issue of congruity does not arise until the individual perceives that there is such a relevant connection between his attitudes toward source and object. In effect, when the individual understands that both he and the persuasive source hold attitudes toward the same object, he sees himself in a unit formation with the source. Accordingly, the prediction of attitude change by way of the congruity hypothesis can readily be translated into statements describing balanced triads. Thus:

> If an individual likes a source, he tends to like the objects the source endorses.
> If an individual dislikes a source, he tends to like the object of which the source disapproves.
> If an individual dislikes a source, he tends to dislike the object the source endorses.
> If an individual likes a source, he tends to dislike the object of which the source disapproves.

Although the congruity model focuses on changes in attitudes toward issues, the movement of the individual's evaluation of the presuasive source toward congruency makes clear that there is a mutual influence at work. In general, attitudes toward objects affect attitudes toward sources who approve or disapprove of these objects. The basis of the mutual influence, however, needs to be specified. Can the movement toward congruence of attitude toward object and source be understood in terms of the individual's conception of the real world and rational behavior? According to this view, if the individual holds a positive attitude toward an object, then he should also hold a positive attitude toward one who is associated with that object. By the same token, a negative attitude toward an object should rationally call for a negative evaluation of one who is associated with the object by way of his positive assertions about it. As in the balance tendency, the implicit assumption in the movement of the two attitudes toward congruity is that they lie along a common dimension. Indeed, failure of the attitudes to become congruent is often accompanied by a differentiation of the attitudes by the subject. Thus, "I respect him as a scientist, but when it comes to politics, he is an absolute boob." In support of this rationalistic view of the congruity model, there are two rationality factors which restrict the amount of congruity pressure or the respective amount of change in the attitudes toward source and object. One, which we have already discussed, is the polarization of the attitudes, which affects resistance to change. The polarization of an attitude may be thought of as a degree of belief or confidence in it. The more polarized an attitude, the more correct the individual thinks it is; hence, the less it tends to move toward congruence with the other attitude. The less polarized the attitude and the less confident the individual about its correctness, the more it is likely to move to the point of consistency with the other attitude.

The second constraint on attitude change is the factor of credulity. When there is a large discrepancy between the individual's existing attitude toward an object and his evaluation of the persuasive source, the congruity pressure apparently weakens or disappears altogether. What happens is that the individual becomes suspicious or utterly disbelieves the communicator. If, for instance, an individual who holds an extremely low opinion of a new club member hears that a respected confrere warmly admires the new member, he is likely to reject what he has heard as a rumor. The same kind of reaction would occur if a well-informed subject in an experiment was told that General Eisenhower had just come out foursquare for increased federal spending on welfare programs. Credulity with respect to the assertions of the persuasive source is a necessary condition for the operation of the model. Furthermore, the amount of congruity pressure generated by an attitude discrepancy is affected by the degree of credulity in the source's communications to the subject.

A different view concerning the basis of congruity pressure is that there is a tendency in human thinking toward maximum simplicity. Congruence between attitudes toward object and source is simpler to maintain than distinctions between them. Related to this type of simplification is the tendency of attitudes to become increasingly polarized. Intuitively, there is no question but that incongruous attitudes require more attention than uniform ones. On the other hand, uniform attitudes can often lead to complications in interpersonal relations. If a young man is introduced by his fiancée to her attractive sister, the congruity pressures operating on his evaluations of the two girls may lead to a great deal of difficulty, at least up to the point when he begins differentiating the basis of his evaluations.

THE DISSONANCE MODEL

The dissonance model of Festinger (1957) is considerably more general than either of the two models already discussed. It does not confine itself to the attitude-change setting as does the congruity model. It also appears to deal with a wider range of inconsistencies than the balance model, in which location in or out of a unit formation is the main basis for predicting whether the evaluation of social and nonsocial objects will become balanced. Although more general than the other models, however, the essential idea of the dissonance model is the same. When cognitions of himself, his actions, and the social and nonsocial environment are mutually inconsistent, a state of dissonance exists for the individual. More technically, when one of a pair of beliefs or evaluations follows from the opposite of the other in the pair, a dissonance exists between the two elements of the pair. When one cognitive element follows from the other, the relation between the two is consonant. Dissonance, like imbalance and incongruity, is negatively motivating; it is a condition which the individual tries to avoid or to reduce.

Considering the empirical applications of the model, the definitions of dissonance are quite diverse. The operational meanings of an obverse relation between cognitions have been illustrated in terms of the type of experimental setup employed. One such paradigm is the situation in which the subject chooses one of several alternatives which vary in attractiveness—for example, objects, betting strategies, or the like. In such a setup, the empirical rule is that, the more attractive the unchosen alternative, the greater the dissonance. In another type of dissonance-producing situation, the individual acts in a manner opposite to the action that would be predicted from the commonly understood meaning of a belief which he holds. The empirical rule in this case is that, the smaller the reward received for the contrary behavior, the greater the dissonance. In a related vein, the more the contrary behavior issues from a voluntary choice of the individual, or the less coercion is required to produce the contrary behavior, the greater the dissonance. Similarly, the more difficult or painful the behavior relative to the reward for which the behavior is required, the greater the dissonance. These setups can be grouped more generally into a so-called "forced compliance" paradigm because, in order to act in a way contrary to his belief, the person has to be more or less forced by way of reward or threat of punishment. But beyond what it takes to make the subject behave inconsistently, the amount of dissonance is *inversely* related to the amount of reward and punishment. In the attitude-change setting, dissonance is a function of the discrepancy between the attitude position of the subject and the attitude position to which the persuader wants him to change, to the extent that the persuader is attractive and cannot be discredited.

Looking at the kinds of dissonance induced in these method-ological contexts, we find instances of logical inconsistency, violations of moral or cultural norms, differences of opinion, disconfirmations of expectations, self-defeating actions, and many other kinds of disturbing conditions. This variety of empirically distinct dissonance-arousing situations raises the question as to whether the conceptual basis of dissonance is a unitary one or consists of several distinct conceptual constellations. In this connection, given dissonance-inducing setups typically require additional assumptions before actions or attitudes designed to reduce dissonance can be predicted. For instance, when a man believes that smoking is dangerous and continues to smoke, his actions contradict his beliefs. But a state of dissonance can only be assumed if the man does not enjoy risks, does not want to die prematurely, or does not think that he lives a charmed life.

One application of the dissonance model directly relevant to interpersonal attraction was made by Aronson and Mills (1959). They argued that dissonance would be produced if the individual recognized negative aspects in an object which he had striven hard and painfully to obtain. Accordingly, dissonance would be expected to exist between any disliked aspects of group membership and any unpleasantness involved in becoming a member. To reduce this kind of contradiction, the individual can deny or underestimate the unpleasantness, or he can raise the evaluation of the group so as to justify the unpleasantness.

Subjects were college females who either volunteered to join a group discussing sex or elected sex as one of several topics for discussion. In order to vary the unpleasantness involved in be-coming a member, subjects were assigned at random to one of three conditions. In both the *Severe* (unpleasantness) and *Mild* conditions, subjects had to take an embarrassment test in front of the experimenter which would, if passed, admit them to the group. Specifically, in the *Severe* condition, the subjects read aloud a list of obscene words and graphic descriptions of love-making. In the *Mild* condition, subjects recited a list of sexually oriented, but not obscene, words. In a control condition, no initiation procedure was required for membership.

Following the initiation procedures, subjects were told they were acceptable as members of the group. However, since they had not read material for that day's discussion, they would have to listen to the discussion through headphones. Actually, a prepared tape was heard by the subjects. In order to create a dissonant relation with the unpleasant initiation, the discussion which the subjects heard was extremely dull. Thus, for the subjects in the *Severe* condition, there theoretically existed a dissonance between the negative experience of listening to the group and the unpleasantness of the initiation. The results were in line with prediction. The evaluation of the group—both participants and the discussion topic—was most positive for the subjects who had had the most unpleasant initiation, next most positive for the subjects under the *Mild* condition, and least positive for the subjects under the control condition. The assumption applied to this result was that the severe initiation could not be denied or underestimated; hence, dissonance reduction occurred by way of the remaining mode, namely, overestimating the attraction of the group.

One might raise an interpretive question at this point. Although formally accepted into the group following the initiation ceremonies, the subjects who had undergone the most severe test still might have felt that their tenure in the group would continue to be uncertain due to their show of embarrassment. Or being competitive girls, they wanted to appear undaunted by the test and capable of rising to the occasion. The position evaluations, then, could have represented communications to the effect that they were still very much interested in the group. Such a "challenge-and-response" tendency, which was less true for the *Mild* condition and absent in the control subjects, has nothing to do with the sort of inconsistency assumed to give rise to dissonance. But even if the results represent a reaction to the contradiction between initiation and membership, the question remains—why is such an inconsistency so intolerable? One possibility is that, when an unpleasant experience is required in order to join a group, the subject supposes and expects that the group will be very attractive. Such an expectation is based, if not on her own personal experience, on her acquaintance with various maxims like: "good things are hard to come by," "the longer you wait the sweeter it is," "you only get what you pay for," and the like. Now, when she hears the tape which describes a dull discussion, her expectation is threatened with disconfirmation unless she can convince herself that the initiation was not so severe after all. Since the unpleasant initiation is undeniable, she tends to discount the unattractive group discussion as a case of sampling unreliability. In other words, the higher evaluation of the group on the part of the severely initiated subjects represents an affirmation of the validity of their expectations and/or a discounting of presumably unreliable contrary evidence.

Even if it could be supposed that, despite the variety of empirical situations, cognitive inconsistency is the basis of all dissonance effects, it still is necessary to recognize that inconsistency may disturb the individual by way of more than one mechanism. If the individual is oriented toward keeping his cognitions fairly close to reality, the existence of an inconsistency could mean that one or both of the contradictory cognitions are in error. Threat to the veridicality of the cognitive structure is one basis of the motivation to resolve the contradiction. A second, quite different basis is that inconsistent behavior increases the probability of social rejection. Since rational, intelligent behavior is highly valued by other people, the individual tries to reduce or at least conceal his irrationality for fear of losing status and power or even love and security. Holding inconsistent cognitions, then, may threaten the individual's grip on reality or arouse social anxiety or both.

CONCLUSIONS ABOUT CONSISTENCY PRESSURE

According to each of the three cognitive models we have briefly discussed, the individual preserves or restores consistency and harmony among cognitions. In the balance model of Heider (1958), cognized objects which are part of a structural unit consisting of the individual and other persons and objects with which he is connected tend to be evaluated in a uniform way. An individual with a positive self-evaluation tends to evaluate positively one who is similar to him with respect to those characteristics which he likes in himself. In the attitude-change setting to which the congruity model (Osgood & Tannenbaum, 1955) is applicable, the tendency to make evaluations consistent is also notable. If a source whom the individual evaluates positively endorses a stand or approves an object which the individual evaluates negatively, there is a congruity disturbance which motivates changes in the evaluations. The dissonance model, in all its varied applications, is also apparently based on the intolerance of some form of inconsistency. The individual who voluntarily suffers pain and embarrassment, only to find that the goal leaves much to be desired, has behaved inconsistently, and this is disconcerting to him.

The important question, already raised in connection with each of the three models, concerns the basis of the inconsistency effect. Although it is not necessary to be concerned with why the model works—as long as it works successfully—a number of possible explanations have been suggested by the model-builders themselves. In the tradition of Gestalt psychology, balance pressures are generated during the process of organizing into a coherent cognitive structure the stimuli with which the organism is continuously bombarded. According to this view, balance forces are indigenous to the cognitive field. It is not necessary to assume external goals or states to which balance is instrumental. A related conception appears in the suggestion that congruity pressure reflects a basic characteristic of human thinking—a tendency toward maximum simplicity. The movement of attitudes toward an issue and toward a communicator, so that they are consistent with each other and with the position positively or negatively evaluated by the communicator, is presumably a case of the basic trend toward a more primitive cognitive structure. Extreme, all-or-nothing judgments are easier to manipulate in thinking than finely discriminated judgments are. The origin of the inconsistency effect in dissonance experiments has been discussed in a recent book which offers a comprehensive review of this field of research (Brehm & Cohen, 1962). According to these authors, dissonance originates in the preponderance of reinforcements which the individual has received for being consistent in his cognitive, affective, and behavioral responses. In time, the high "payoff" of consistency causes it to become an end in itself. Parents and other child-trainers may in fact reward cognitive consistency directly, so that it could be a motivation in its own right from an early stage of development. As for the contemporaneous basis of dissonance, it is proposed that cognitive inconsistencies are motivating because they frustrate other goals present for the individual. In short, dissonance has its disturbing effect either because it frustrates the need for consistency or because it prevents the satisfaction of other needs.

None of the foregoing formulations is entirely satisfactory. The suggestion that there are autochthonous forces toward a good simple structure (*prägnanz*) in the cognitive field appears to close discussion as to the basis of the inconsistency effect. The idea that dissonance is a frustration leads to the question: How it is frustrating, and why? Finally, to postulate cognitive consistency as a need in itself does not seem to penetrate beneath the surface and leaves open several possibilities.

Two specific bases of the inconsistency effect have already been proposed and need to be carefully distinguished in testing hypotheses about attraction and hostility. 1) Inconsistency is negatively valued in most social environments. If the person acts or expresses an attitude which can be interpreted as inconsistent, he is subject to a more or less severe loss of prestige. To avoid the loss, the individual is inclined either to inhibit inconsistent behavior or to minimize it after it has taken place. From this point of view, it is fear of social censure, ridicule, or rejection which causes change in the evaluation of himself and others so that they are mutually consistent. 2) Inconsistency is a threat to the need of the individual to maintain a close relationship between his cognitive structure and reality. From this point of view, changes in the evaluation of himself and others may be interpreted as attempts to make cognitions as to the worth of himself and others correspond more closely to reality as the individual defines it.

In conclusion, cognitive models do not lead to unique interpretations of attraction and hostility data. The effects of cognitive inconsistency can usually be decomposed into the effects of social motivations, particularly status and security needs, and a cognitive motivation to form and maintain a veridical cognitive structure.

REFERENCES

Aronson, Elliott, and Mills, Judson. "The Effect of Severity of Initiation on Liking for a Group," *Journal of Abnormal and Social Psychology*, XLIX (1959), 177–181.

Brehm, Jack W., and Cohen, Arthur R. *Explorations in Cognitive Dissonance.* New York: Wiley, 1962.

Deutsch, Morton, and Solomon, Leonard. "Reactions to Evaluations by Others as Influenced by Self-Evaluations," *Sociometry*, XXII (1959), 93–112.

Festinger, Leon. *A Theory of Cognitive Dissonance.* Evanston, Ill.: Row Peterson, 1957,

Festinger, Leon, and Hutte, Herman A. "An Experimental Investigation of the Effects of Unstable Interpersonal Relations in a Group," *Journal of Abnormal and Social Psychology*, XLIX (1954), 513–522.

Heider, Fritz. *The Psychology of Interpersonal Relations.* New York: Wiley, 1958.

Newcomb, Theodore M. "An Approach to the Study of Communicative Acts," *Psychological Review*, LX (1953), 393–404.

Osgood, C., and Tannenbaum, H. "The Principle of Congruity in the Prediction of Attitude Change," *Psychological Review*, LXII (1955), 42–55.

3 Cognitive Motivation in Social Behavior

It has already been proposed that a purely cognitive interpretation of attraction and hostility can be made by assuming a "validation" motive—a need of the individual to maintain a cognitive structure which correctly maps physical or social reality concerning the value of himself and others along some dimension. Generally implied by this formulation is that whenever an estimate of his own or another person's worth deviates from estimates of an objective valuation in a given respect, the individual will tend to change his cognitive structure so that such valuations are more in line with reality. Before looking at experimental data which is exclusively concerned with attraction and hostility, however, it will be useful to evaluate the evidence for a validation or similar cognitive motivational process in other areas of

50

social behavior. Such an analysis will not only permit a judgment about the generality of the hypothesis, but will also provide information as to the kinds of experimental controls needed to test attraction and hostility hypotheses.

CONFORMITY IN PHYSICAL JUDGMENTS

In his classical experiments with the autokinetic phenomenon, Sherif (1936) appeared to demonstrate a cognitive basis for social conformity in making physical judgments. It is well known that when an individual fixates a pinpoint source of light in an otherwise dark room, the light appears to him to waver and move. The physical basis of such an illusion is the lack of structure or framework necessary to localize the light in space. In one part of his experiments, Sherif found that the estimates of light movement which subjects had made privately tended to converge—to become more like those of the other subjects— when they were vocalized in each other's presence. One way of interpreting this result is to assume that conformity in making judgments represents a means of establishing a reliable estimate of how much light movement actually appeared. A relatively uniform distribution of judgments represents a social norm which can function as a substitute for physical reality. In Sherif's terms, the judgments of the entire group of subjects provided a needed frame of reference within which any individual could place his judgments. More specifically, such findings are consistent with the idea that the unstructured stimulus situation aroused a cognitive-validation need and that the tendency toward agreement with others functioned, at least in part, as a means of bringing about a truer cognitive structure with respect to stimulus movement. However, despite its plausible appeal, such an interpretation is by no means unequivocal. It is possible that part of the trend toward agreement among subjects in the estimated amount of light movement was based on their fear of being humiliated or rejected, or, in general, of losing status and security. In other words, the convergence of judgments in the group situation could be produced by either a "reality-mapping" process or a social motivation or both.

Not only can these two possibilities contribute to the conformity effect independently, but they can, and likely do, interact in subtle ways. For example, the more unstructured a
stimulus situation for a given subject, the more correct he thinks
others can be, and the more wrong he thinks he can be. Thus,
although unstructuredness may arouse a need for a veridical
cognitive structure with respect to light movement, it may also
intensify anxiety over being regarded as ignorant or insensitive.
Unless the subject knows or can infer that, for the others in
the group, the stimulus situation is equally unstructured, a social
motivation is likely to be confounded with a cognitive-validation
need. Furthermore, assuming there is no way to obtain a cognitive structure of reality through objective or quasi-objective
means, the more unstructured the physical-stimulus situation,
the more one is dependent on others for obtaining such a veridical picture. The hypothetical cognitive-validation need, then, is
satisfied through social means, and the social motivation is
strongly affected by cognitive factors. Consequently, the observation that conformity varies with the degree of unstructuredness
in the stimulus situation does not permit a decision as to the
motivational basis of such behavior.

In Asch's well-known experiment dealing with the judgment
of lines (1960), both cognitive and social motivations were involved. Subjects had the specific task of selecting one of three
comparison lines which most closely matched in length a standard line. Unknown to him, each of the several confederates who
vocalized their judgments prior to his response gave the wrong
answer on a certain number of trials according to plan. When
this occurred, the subject presumably was placed in a dilemma
as to whether to disobey the instructions of his senses, on which
he presumably depended for information about the real world,
or to deviate from the consensus of his fellow students and
thereby run the risk of being ridiculed or rejected. The outcome
—in terms of conformity—appeared to depend upon the relative strength of the reality-matching tendency and the social
motivations involved.

Actually, the conflict was probably not quite so simple. The finding that two-thirds of the judgments were "independent," despite the "pressure" of the majority, does not necessarily demonstrate a cognitive-validation need. Subjects, after all, were instructed to select the correct alternative. There might well have been a fear of incurring the displeasure of the experimenter or a desire to please him and help his experiments succeed. On the other hand, conformity to the majority judgment cannot be assumed to rest exclusively on fear of being ridiculed and thought different by the majority. It is likely that, for some subjects, the majority response was actually considered the correct response. As in the autokinetic experiment discussed above, the majority was probably considered a source of reality by some subjects.

To understand the dynamics of conformity and independence in making physical judgments, it is necessary to isolate the component forces which constitute the conflict. Accordingly, in the same kind of setup used in the Asch studies, Deutsch and Gerard (1955) tried to eliminate the role of social motivations. They divided their subjects into two groups: those who made their judgments in a situation where they could not be identified as individuals and those who responded publicly. As expected, the subjects who made their judgments privately and anonymously showed much less conformity. Apparently, the subjects could stick by their senses and/or follow the implied experimental instructions to make correct judgments without much fear of reprisal from the other subjects. One can conclude that independent judgments were not produced by a threatened loss of status or security, but there is nothing conclusive to show what their motivational basis actually was.

A finding of further interest in the Asch experiments was that, when the standard and comparison lines were objectively similar in length—that is, when it was more difficult to determine what the correct response was—there was greater conformity. This tends to support the cognitive interpretation of the experiment: Stimulus equivocality arouses a cognitive-validation need and increases the individual's dependence on the social environment to satisfy it. However, such a result can also support a social-motivational interpretation that equivocality increases the likelihood of error and, hence, the possibility that the individual will be regarded as incompetent.

Still another result of these fruitful studies is relevant to the question of a cognitive-validation motivation. Within rather definite limits, as the size of the majority increased, the amount of conformity increased. One interpretation is that, from the subject's point of view, the sheer number of persons comprising the norm affects its reliability and validity as a criterion for estimating the correct line lengths. When two persons make a credible assertion, it is more likely to be accepted as true than when only one person makes the same assertion. If such a result was observed in private, where the subject could respond without fear of social punishment, the cognitive interpretation would be strengthened. A public response, however, could mean that the severity of a status threat increases with the size of the majority.

OPINION CONFORMITY

With respect to the dynamics of opinion formation and change, Festinger (1950) made explicit what was implicit in Sherif's earlier work in the area of physical judgments. He proposed that individuals have a need to validate—to establish the truth of—their opinions. When a difference of opinion occurs and there is no objective standard available, there is a tendency for individuals to seek agreement with others. Such uniformity serves as a social standard for the verification of opinions. For many of the reasons already discussed, however, it has been difficult to confirm this cognitive, "social-reality" hypothesis experimentally.

An experiment by Festinger, Gerard, Hymovitch, Kelley, and Raven (1952) attempted to check a key implication of the hypothesis. If opinion conformity stems from a need to validate opinions, providing the individual with potential resources for objective validation—that is, reducing his dependence on the social environment—should affect his conformity or his behavior designed to make others conform. Two variables which theoretically might affect social dependence were manipulated in a setup where subjects were given to believe there was a difference of opinion among them concerning a labor-management problem. Under one experimental condition, subjects were told there were experts on labor-management problems present in the group. Under such circumstances, it was thought that subjects would not require uniformity in the opinion of the group as a whole to establish the validity of their opinions. Rather, they would need to agree only with those whom they guessed to be experts. In the aggregate, this would lead to fewer attempts to influence others in order to bring about uniformity. In fact, fewer interpersonal communications were found under most of the "expert-present" conditions. In a second experimental condition, subjects were led to believe that a correct answer existed for the labor-management problem. Here again, although in a different form, there was a potential means for the objective verification of opinions and, therefore, less social dependence for the satisfaction of the cognitive need presumably operating. A general trend toward fewer communicated words was shown under these conditions.

Although such findings are consistent with the assumption of a reality-mapping process, they can also be explained by reference to a social motivation. Thus, when there are experts in the group, or when there is a right answer, individuals tend to fear that they would lose personal status if it became known that they possessed the wrong answer. Clearly, such a threat of status loss could well lead to restraint in communicating with others.

COMPETITIVE COALITION FORMATION

The assumption that individuals need to validate their opinions was extended by Festinger (1954) to the realm of abilities. It was proposed that individuals have a need to find out how much ability they have. Since, in general, there are no completely objective tests, the individual tends to evaluate his ability according to what relevant others think of it or in terms of how his performance compares with that of others whose performance he considers to represent a relevant standard. By changing his performance so that it is equal to the performance of others with whom he compares himself, the individual correctly evaluates his ability.

Hoffman, Festinger, and Lawrence (1954) tested an implication regarding the boundary conditions of the hypothetical self-assessment need. They argued that, when others' abilities are perceived to be too different from the subject's own, he will show a reduced tendency to form competitive coalitions for ability-evaluation purposes. Where the discrepancy in ability precludes comparison, the individual tends to acknowledge superiority or inferiority, as the case may be. Two subjects and a confederate who posed as a subject constructed geometric figures. The points to be gained by assembling the pieces correctly were to contribute to the subjects' IQ. Each participant started out with parts of the figure and could trade with the others to obtain the required parts. Actual bargaining was permitted, and coalitions could be formed between two participants against the third in order to pool resources and gain point advantages. In one experimental condition, the two subjects were led to believe that the confederate was a natively superior individual, whereas, in another condition, he was presented as having the same intellectual caliber. In both conditions, it was arranged that the confederate enjoyed a constant lead in number of points. As expected, subjects formed more coalitions with each other against the confederate when the latter was described as their equal than when he was described as a basically superior person. Since all other things were equal in the two conditions, it presumably was the discrepancy in ability which accounted for the variations in the tendency to compete against the confederate. When this discrepancy was large and irreversible, the subjects ceased to compete and acknowledged the confederate's superiority. On the other hand, where subjects thought they were more or less equal in ability, they formed coalitions in order to keep the confederate's performance comparable to their own.

Despite the results, which are consistent with a validation hypothesis in the area of abilities, social motivations cannot be decisively eliminated as determinants of competitive coalition formation. Individuals who are motivated to achieve status or who fear losing it are expressly concerned with beating competitors. The fact that there was less competitive coalition formation against those who were judged to be superior could simply reflect the fact that status motivation is affected by the probability of success and failure. The dependence of competitive tendencies upon the relative superiority of adversaries does not necessarily and exclusively confirm the assumption of a need to evaluate one's own abilities correctly.

LEVEL OF ASPIRATION

The setting of goals according to their difficulty can also be interpreted in terms of the ability-validation hypothesis. An experiment by Dreyer (1954) dealt with the question of how long a subject continues to set levels of aspiration as a function of the discrepancy between his performance and that of a reference group of peers. Subjects performed a card-sorting task and were divided into three experimental groups. In one, the subject was told that his performance was average for his peer group. In the second, the subject's performance was reported to be superior to that of his peers, and in the third, inferior to the same extent. The results show that the spontaneous cessation of aspiration occurred on a significantly earlier trial in the condition where the subjects were *above* the norm. There was not a significant difference, however, between the *Average-* and *Low-Performance* subjects. These findings could be interpreted only partly in line with the predication based on the ability-validation hypothesis. Thus, the *High-Performance* subjects regarded themselves as noncomparable with the peer group; they acknowledged themselves as superior and stopped aspiring. The hypothesis also predicted, however, that the subjects whose performance was relatively low would acknowledge their inferiority and stop aspiring at the same time as the superior subjects. To account for the *Low-Performance* subjects' continued setting of goals, it was proposed that the cognitive drive is often complicated by a status-achievement or avoidance-of-failure motivation. Accordingly, although the *Low-Performance* subjects had no need to continue to aspire from the standpoint of validating their abilities, they did persist in setting levels of aspiration on the basis of the status drive directed upward.

The motivation to achieve status or to avoid the loss of it may also account, at least in part, for the *High-Performance* subjects' stopping first. As in the coalition experiment described above, status motivation may be affected by probabilities of success and failure. If the chances of losing status are zero, competitive drive may be attenuated on the grounds that the battle is already won.

AFFILIATION TENDENCIES

One important measure of interpersonal attraction is the degree to which individuals seek the company of others. In recent years, a number of experiments have attempted to isolate the determinants of such affiliation tendencies. A detailed analysis of these studies is an essential introduction to our own studies in the attraction-hostility area. On the basis of an integrated series of investigations, Schachter (1959) proposed that a self-evaluation motivation could account partially for the individual's stated preference to affiliate with other subjects when he is faced with a potentially dangerous experience. Strong fear was aroused in groups of subjects by leading them to expect a severe electric shock in the experiment to follow later. Other groups of subjects were told they would receive weak shocks. Subjects were then asked to record on prepared forms whether they would prefer to wait for the experiment to begin with the others who had received the same fear-arousing instructions or go off to a room and wait by themselves. It was found that strong fear was significantly associated with the stated desire to affiliate. A further study showed that preference for affiliation on the part of subjects who feared the shock held up even under conditions where subjects were told they would not be permitted to talk to each other. The cumulative results of several experiments suggested two bases for affiliation: reduction of fear through obtaining some form of comfort and protection and/or validation of the emotional state (fear) aroused by the anticipation of a painful shock. The latter interpretation is based on the hypothesis that individuals need to know whether their emotional reactions are valid in the sense of being commensurate with or qualitatively appropriate to the conditions which aroused them. In other words, individuals need to validate their feelings just as they do their opinions and abilities. Since, generally speaking, the raw physiological experience of emotion does not provide sufficiently detailed information about its appropriateness, individuals seek validating information by observing the reactions of others to the same stimulus conditions.

In order to obtain more precise information relevant to these theoretical interpretations, an experiment was carried out (Wrightsman, 1960) in which actual affiliation was permitted following the arousal of fear. In this study, subjects were told individually that they would receive injections which not only were painful, but would have unpleasant aftereffects. Following this anxiety-arousing procedure, subjects rated their level of uneasiness and were assigned to one of three experimental conditions: a condition in which they waited alone for five minutes; a condition in which they waited for five minutes with three other subjects; or an identical "together" condition, but with a prohibition against talking. The experiment concluded with a second self-rating of the subject's anxiety. The results showed that affiliation produced a general reduction in the subject's self-ratings of fear. For one category of subjects (only or first-born children), the fear reduction was significantly greater for the affiliators than the isolates, whether the former could talk to each other or not. In addition, the level of fear became more uniform as a consequence of affiliation, again regardless of whether talk was allowed or not. Some subjects, who had been very fearful before associating with each other, now rated themselves as less fearful; others, initially unafraid, were very fearful after being together with the others. This increased homogenization of fear ratings suggests that a social-influence process took place and, thus, that affiliation was determined by and actually resulted in an emotional validation.

It should be noted that such a cognitive interpretation involves the implicit assumption that the emotions which are aroused lack validity in some dimension. However, in the case of the particular emotional states aroused in these experiments—fear of shock or fear of an injection and its consequences—it is difficult to suppose that subjects were ignorant of their feelings and the basis of them. Subjects knew that they were going to be shocked or injected, they presumably knew that these events were responsible for their being anxious, and, most likely, they had experienced such fears or similar ones before. It is true that the experimental setting, including the behavior and appearance of the experimenter, were strange and novel for them, but the emotion of fear and its causation seemed to have been clear enough.

A second interpretive problem arises from the possibility that subjects wish to avoid embarrassment, humiliation, and loss of status generally. In the interaction situation, it is possible that a norm concerning the socially proper amount of fear was developed on the basis of such a social motivation. Those who were initially afraid came to feel that others would think they were being excessively weak and infantile; those who were unafraid felt they would be regarded as rather unemotional. The important point here is that such a social norm need not have had anything to do with emotional validation. As for the affiliation preference on the part of subjects who were threatened with shock, again social pressures might have been operating, at least in the study where subjects recorded their preferences in full view of each other. Perhaps, for example, it was felt that waiting alone would be interpreted as a sign of immaturity—indeed of being thought overly afraid. Or, it may have been that the subjects did not know what was the socially proper thing to do when faced with the prospect described by the experimenter. By affiliating and observing the reactions of others they could find out. This general line of interpretation, then, although not cognitive, would predict increased uniformity in the ratings reflecting fear, just as it would predict uniformities in judgments or opinions.

If affiliation on the part of a fearful subject is based on his need to validate his emotional state, supplying the subject with objective information concerning his fear should reduce the tendency. Following this logic, Gerard and Rabbie (1961) designed an experiment in which the subjects could be informed about the intensity of their own and their partners' reactions to anticipated shock. Specifically, subjects in whom either a high or low level of such fear was induced were led to believe that the electrodes attached to their arms measured the degree of emotional reaction. In one experimental condition, each subject received information about his own degree of arousal by way of a microammeter facing him in his cubicle. In a second treatment, the subject received microammeter information about his own reaction and the reactions of the other three subjects. The dial representing his own reaction, of course, pointed to the same number in the two conditions. In a third treatment, the subject was given no information about the level of his or anyone else's reaction. Following these information manipulations, subjects were asked whether they wanted to wait with the others for the experiment to begin or wait alone in a separate room. Subjects also rated the strength of their desire to wait alone or wait together.

In all, only a little over 10 per cent of the subjects chose to be alone, and these were randomly distributed over the treatments. However, the affiliation ratings of those who chose to be together yielded results germane to the emotional-validation hypothesis. In all three information conditions, high fear produced stronger affiliation ratings than low fear. At both levels of fear, subjects who were made aware of their own *and* their partners' reactions had the weakest desire to affiliate. Subjects who were given information only about their own reaction had the strongest desire—even stronger than those who were given no information at all.

The results of the information treatments appear to partially support the emotional-validation hypothesis, but there are two specific sources of potential embarrassment to it. If the subject believes that the information describing his own emotional reaction is valid, his need for emotional validation should presumably be satisfied. Giving him additional information about his partners' reactions should not bring about any further reduction in the strength of his desire to affiliate. Yet, the results show a significantly weaker desire to affiliate on the part of subjects who knew both their own and their partners' reactions. Actually, this finding need not be embarrassing to the validation hypothesis. For one thing, the intensity of an emotion is not the only dimension on which validation is needed. For complete validation, one would want information about the meaning of the emotion, the qualitative aspects of the emotional experience, its behavioral or expressive implications, and so on. Although an excellent source of validation regarding the intensity of the emotion, the subject's dial reading did not provide information about these other aspects. However, the information concerning the arousal of the other three persons, especially when comparable with that about his own feelings, could have provided a relatively more complete validation. Secondly, the information given the subject about the intensity of his own emotional state might not have been considered perfectly reliable. (The subject's retrospective estimate of what he had thought the dial reading would be in terms of the same scale rarely agreed exactly with the actual dial reading.) Thus, the subject who had an approximate idea of his own emotional reaction could still have had a strong motivation to validate his emotion by a social comparison. Information about how his emotional intensity compared with that of others could have been expected to provide such validation.

The more troublesome finding is that the condition in which the subject knows the intensity of his own emotional state shows a mean affiliation strength which is higher than that in the condition in which no information at all is given. If an emotional-validation need is a determinant of the strength of desire to affiliate, then the complete absence of validating information ought to make the desire strongest. The possibility exists, however, that, when an individual possesses no information, he does not know which aspect of himself needs validation. On the other hand, the person who knows his own reaction also knows what might require further validation. More generally, it can be said that, when an emotional reaction is extremely diffuse and unexplainable by reference to the stimulus situation, it either becomes difficult to validate through social comparison, or social comparison is regarded as ineffective altogether. In line with this possibility, it should be noted that subjects were in booths isolated from each other from the outset. This design feature was a decided improvement over the original procedure employed by Schachter (1959), where the arousal of fear and the statement of the "together" or "alone" possibilities were accomplished with the subjects in full view of one another. But although separating subjects presumably ruled out direct social influence in the subject's choice of "together" or "alone," it also reduced the various cues which enabled him to obtain even an elementary grasp of the situation.

A second possibility is that having no information about his own reaction lessens the individual's desire for affiliation because he anticipates criticism and rejection when found to be ignorant. This interpretation would be likely if the subject was not sure what information the other subjects were getting or, in general, what the state of their knowledge was. In the two information conditions, the subject presumably did know that the other subjects were receiving the same type of information that he was. In the no-information condition, however, the subject might have judged the others to be better informed and, thus, might have been reluctant to associate with them. A social motivation, in short, could have accounted for the relatively weak affiliation tendency.

By varying the adequacy of groups as providers of opinion validation, Radloff (1961) also tested a cognitive hypothesis of affiliation. As part of an opinion survey, subjects indicated their positions on an educational issue and were then shown a particular comparison group's distribution of opinions on the same topic. Following the validation opportunity made available by

such normative information, subjects checked one of four statements reflecting the strength of their desire to join a discussion
group on the problem of education. The expectation was that
the affiliation tendency would depend on the ability of the
group to provide information which could validate the subject's
opinion, as well as on the position of the subject in relation
to the modal opinion of the comparison group. In connection
with the latter, a large discrepancy would preclude comparison.
A control condition in which the subject received *no* normative
information should result in the least amount of validation and,
hence, the maximum need for affiliation. University-student subjects, given information about the opinions of high-school sopho-
mores, should be expected to receive more validation than those
who received no information, but still a negligible amount from
this relatively ignorant group. Information on the subjects' peer
group should presumably provide more validation, and information about the opinions of "experts," including university presi-
dents, should provide maximum validation for the subjects'
opinions. The prediction of an increasing affiliation tendency
with a decrease in the validation presumably obtained from the
four comparison conditions was confirmed.

ASSESSMENT OF COGNITIVE HYPOTHESES

Let us summarize the evidence for and against the interpretation of various social behaviors in terms of a need of the individual to form and maintain a cognitive structure which correctly maps reality.

First, when physical judgments are made in a group setting,
there is a close relation between the degree of unstructuredness
of the stimulus and the degree to which the individual conforms
to the judgments of the group, even when the group, according
to experimental design, makes incorrect judgments. This general
finding would seem to indicate that, when physical reality is
impoverished or absent altogether, the individual tends to rely
on social norms to keep his judgments in line with reality. Unstructuredness, however, may also threaten the individual if he
expects that others will personally devalue him if he should

expose his ignorance. Consequently, the conformity observed under unstructured or equivocal stimulus conditions may be based, at least in part, on fear of loss of status or security.

Second, in a situation where individuals hold different opinions, behavior designed to bring about uniformity, namely, verbal communication, is affected by the ability of the social environment to provide a definition of reality. Specifically, if subjects are told that there are experts in the group or that there is a correct answer, there tends to be a drop in their level of social communication. But a drop in communication under such circumstances could be due to the subjects' fear that expressing the wrong opinion would result in their being criticized or otherwise devalued.

Third, in a bargaining situation, the frequency and strength of coalitions which two subjects form against a confederate depends upon whether the latter is an intellectual peer or a basically superior person. When one player in a bargaining situation is thought to be definitely higher in intelligence than the other players, fewer coalitions are formed against him, presumably because he is beyond a reasonable range of comparison. A large ability discrepancy makes it difficult or impossible to assess one's true ability. But if one assumes that players are motivated to win points and to obtain all the social prestige that comes with winning, then their lack of competitiveness may simply reflect their pessimism over the chances of winning when dealing with a superior adversary. To try and then to lose is a bigger loss of status than to acknowledge the other player's superiority at the start.

Fourth, in a situation where subjects are fearful of being shocked, affiliation is preferred to being alone, even under conditions where no communication of any kind is allowed. Moreover, there is evidence of a greater uniformity in the self-ratings of fear after a short period of actual interaction. This picture of a social-influence process is consistent with the assumption that individuals need to determine the meaning of their feelings and do so by observing the reactions of others in the same situation. But the development of social norms with respect to ratings reflecting emotional states may be based on social motivations, such as anxiety over being regarded as excessively fearful or excessively cool. Similarly, the tendency to remain with others while waiting for the experiment to begin could be based on a fear of being personally devalued by others for being antisocial.

Fifth, when a subject is given information about the intensity of his own and his partners' emotional reactions to a dangerous stimulus, the strength of his desire to affiliate is less than if he receives information about only his own reaction. This finding seems to support the hypothesis that the individual validates his emotional states by observing the reactions of others. It must be assumed, however, that objective information about only his own emotional state does not completely validate it and that information about the other subjects' emotional states adds to the validation obtained. There is also the curious finding that individuals with no information whatsoever have a weak desire to affiliate—less than, instead of more than, subjects who receive information about their own reactions. This plainly contradicts the emotional-validation interpretation, unless it can be assumed that emotional states aroused in a completely isolated individual with no contextual cues with which to construct a meaning are interpreted as so unique and private that no validation is possible. Or it also might be the case that an isolated subject who is fed no information tends to assume that others have more information than he has. He is reluctant to affiliate because he does not want to expose his ignorance.

Sixth, when an individual receives information on the opinions of members of other groups with respect to a subject on which he has taken a stand, his opinion can be validated to the extent that the group is relevant. Thus, groups of experts are able to provide more validation than groups of persons who are less educated on the issue. The more the individual's opinion is validated through information provided by comparison groups, the less his need to affiliate for purposes of validation.

In summary, the evidence that a cognitive-validation need determines various social behaviors is impressive but not conclusive. In some studies, we cannot be sure that such a need was operating and, even if present, whether it was confounded with a social motivation. In the experiments which demonstrated social conformity in the making of physical judgments, neither lack of information about the nature of the stimulus nor difficulty in comprehending it necessarily arouses a cognitve-validation need. Although it can be said that the subject does not know with any degree of certainty what the true nature of the stimulus is, equally, he is not certain that his interpretation of the stimulus departs from reality. Moreover, unstructured and equivocal stimulus situations are capable of arousing social motivations, particularly status threats. Similarly, the establishment of an opinion discrepancy does not necessarily mean that the individual thinks his opinion is invalid or even that he is uncertain of its validity. A difference between the individual's performance and that of a relevant group likewise does not necessarily imply that he is uncertain as to his true ability. Furthermore, opinion and performance discrepancies may generate social motivations, and the presence of these may make it difficult to assign an exclusive explanatory role to opinion- and ability-validation tendencies. Concerning the emotional-validation hypothesis, the problem is that the emotional state which is experimentally aroused does not necessarily lack validity. The individual may very well understand his emotional state and recognize that it is appropriate to the given circumstances.

Briefly, Part I suggests the conclusion that neither the need-satisfaction nor the cognitive-consistency model is sufficiently precise for making detailed statements about the data of attraction and hostility.

Second, theoretical interpretations of these data—for example, experimental findings on cohesiveness and aggression—which are based on the dynamics of specific social motives like status and security do account more adequately than the global models for the concrete research data of these fields. But in many, if not in all, instances where such interpretations are proposed, it is possible to supply an alternative interpretation based on the assumption of a cognitive-validation process.

Third, an analysis of research results bearing on conformity, level of aspiration, coalition formation, and other behaviors along the broad spectrum of social psychology appears to lend support to the assumption of a validation or similar cognitive process as an underlying explanatory construct. However, such a conclusion is not unequivocal. In almost every case where experimental data are given a cognitive interpretation, the intrusion of status- and security-achievement and -defensive processes seems probable. To test validation hypotheses regarding attraction and hostility, therefore, requires experimental designs in which threats and promises of loss and gain in status and security are held constant or eliminated altogether.

REFERENCES

Asch, Solomon. "Effects of Group Pressure Upon the Modification and Distortion of Judgments," in Dorwin Cartwright and Alvin Zander, eds., *Group Dynamics: Research and Theory*. Chicago: Row Peterson, 1960.

Deutsch, Morton, and Gerard, Harold B. "A Study of Normative and Informational Social Influences Upon Individual Judgment," *Journal of Abnormal and Social Psychology*, LI (1955), 629–636.

Dreyer, Albert S. "Aspiration Behavior as Influenced by Expectation and Group Comparison," *Human Relations*, VII (1954), 175–190.

Festinger, Leon. "Informal Social Communication," *Psychological Review*, LVII (1950), 271–281.

Festinger, Leon, *et al.* "The Influence Process in the Presence of Extreme Deviates," *Human Relations*, V (1952), 327–346.

Gerard, Harold B., and Rabbie, Jacob M. "Fear and Social Comparison," *Journal of Abnormal and Social Psychology*, LXII (1961), 586–592.

Hoffman, Paul J., Festinger, Leon, and Lawrence, Douglas H. "Tendencies Toward Group Comparability in Competitive Bargaining," *Human Relations*, VII (1954), 141–159.

Radloff, Roland. "Opinion Evaluation and Affiliation," *Journal of Abnormal and Social Psychology*, LXII (1961), 578–585.

Schachter, Stanley. *The Psychology of Affiliation*. Stanford, Calif.: Stanford University Press, 1959.

Sherif, Muzafer. *The Psychology of Social Norms*. New York: Harper, 1936.

Wrightsman, L. S. "Effects of Waiting With Others on Changes in Level of Felt Anxiety," *Journal of Abnormal and Social Psychology*, LXI (1960), 216–222.

II Empirical Explorations

INTRODUCTION TO PART II

Before examining specific experimental hypotheses and designs, it is necessary to indicate more precisely the kind of data in the field of attraction and hostility with which our research program is concerned. It is clear from even a cursory review of the research literature that operational indicators of attraction and hostility have been highly diverse. Interpersonal attraction, including group cohesiveness, for example, has been assumed to be reflected by choice of partners for given tasks, stated desire to affiliate with others, ratings on how much others are liked, various projective measures on the subject's spontaneous desire to belong or his fear of rejection, and so on. Measures of hostility, notably those used in experiments on aggression, have also been heterogeneous. Aggression has been assumed to be reflected by verbal criticism, delivery of shock to the partner, drawings which depict physical injury, attributions of undesirable personality traits, projective tests, and many other devices and behaviors.

Although manifestly varied, many of these measures of attraction and hostility have the common property of being *evaluations* which individuals make of others or of themselves along one or more dimensions such as ability, moral character, and personality. The evaluations are either explicit, such as when a subject characterizes the experimenter as a "lunkhead," or inferable from attitudes and actions such as when a child decapitates a doll which is represented as "Mother." We do not propose that *all* phenomena apparently under the rubric of attraction and hostility are reducible to positive or negative evaluations. There are doubtful cases, such as when a boy kicks a can down the street. This behavior could be displaced aggression, brought on by his teacher's criticism of him, or a fantasy of getting the can past the goalie, stimulated by a hockey game seen the previous evening. In neither case is there a palpable evaluation of the can as such. Nonetheless, a substantial number of the operational measures of interpersonal aggression, cohesiveness, and other subdivisions of attraction and hostility can readily be characterized as positive and negative evaluations. This partial, working conceptualization of attraction and hostility has the advantage of bringing together for analysis, in terms of the same causal dynamics, these two classes of phenomena which, by historical accident, have been treated separately.

The research problem before us, then, is to confirm that a cognitive-validation process is a determinant of social and self-evaluations and to specify, in as much detail as possible, the conditions under which it operates. In general, the condition for identifying a validation need is the perception by the individual that an estimate of another person's (or his own) valuation along some dimension is invalid according to standards which, for him, represent objective reality. If there exists a validation need and other motives are weaker or absent, the individual should tend to reject or modify the invalid estimate in order to achieve and maintain a valid cognitive structure. His observed evaluations of others and of himself, in part, reflect the hypothetical validation process.

Concrete conditions for arousing a validation need appear to be met in the simple and frequent everyday circumstance in which an individual interacts with another person who is boastful. When this person expresses a self-evaluation in some area which is more positive than a subject finds warranted by reference to criteria of the person's objective worth in that area, the subject should be expected to reject the invalid self-estimate. This process of rejecting the person's invalid self-estimate should be reflected in negative evaluations of him. In Chapter 4, a study is described in which a boastful personality is experimentally created in order to follow up this theoretical lead. In Chapter 5, a quantitative test of the validation hypothesis is made. The discrepancy between a person's implied opinion of himself and an estimate of his objective worth is experimentally manipulated in order to see whether the subject's evaluation of the person corresponds to the size of the discrepancy. In Chapter 6, a further implication of the hypothesized validation process is examined. If negative evaluations of other persons are, in part, determined by the perception of invalid overestimates of their worth, positive evaluations should be determined by the opposite condition. Thus, if another person's self-estimate is lower than it ought to be according to standards which the subject accepts as objective, the evaluations of this person should be more positive than those of a person whose self-estimate is about "right." Chapter 7 deals with a somewhat differently slanted test of the basic validation hypothesis. The question is posed: How is the evaluation of another person affected by the positive or negative bias of an informant who describes that person?

As already mentioned, the tendency to validate evaluations of others should also apply to the self. When the individual's estimate of his true worth in some area comes to differ from his previously existing self-estimate, there is a tendency for him to change the latter in the direction of greater validity. Thus, self-evaluations are, in part, reflections of the hypothetical self-validation process. Manipulation of an individual's estimate of his own worth, however, often involves the simultaneous arousal of his self-esteem motivation. If, for example, an individual is persuaded that his true valuation—for example, in ability—is lower than he thought it was, the tendency for him to lower his self-evaluation conflicts with the tendency for him to maintain his self-esteem. The analysis and prediction of self-evaluation, then, are based on the outcome of a self-evaluation *conflict*. Chapter 8 describes a preliminary experiment on the outcome of a self-evaluation conflict which was created by getting the subject to violate self-relevant norms. Chapter 9 tests specific hypotheses concerning the conditions which determine the direction in which a self-evaluation conflict is resolved. Chapter 10 tests a hypothesis about the effect of a self-evaluation conflict on "projection"—the attribution of positive and negative personality characteristics to others relative to the self. Chapter 11 investigates the hypothesis that the reward which an individual will compete for in a two-person game tends to be that amount which will confirm and validate his estimate of his own worth.

It should be mentioned, finally, that the statistical analyses performed on the data are parametric or nonparametric, depending upon the characteristics of the distribution and measurement scales which the given data describe. In the interests of conservative theoretical statements, two-tailed tests are used, except where hypotheses are explicitly directional.

4 The Reaction to Boastfulness

In studies designed to arouse aggression, the instigator often not only threatens the subject, but also expresses an extremely high self-evaluation. Subjects are insulted about their intelligence, sexual attractiveness, and character, and, at the same time, the instigator implies or explicitly describes his own superiority in these respects. Such a circumstance suggests that whatever aggressive actions and attitudes the subject displays might reflect a cognitive-validation process in addition to, or perhaps instead of, a reaction to the threat of a loss in status or security. Thus, if there is evidence of a discrepancy between the self-esteem expressed by the instigator and his estimated true worth, an individual can be expected to reject the estimate implied by the boastfulness. In most aggression studies, various criteria representing the objective worth of the instigator along certain dimensions are typically available to the subject. There is, for example, the absolute level of the instigator's self-evaluation itself. An extremely positive self-estimate in a given area probably belies the instigator's true worth in that area. The subject reacts: "No one is that good." The expressed confidence of the instigator also supplies clues as to the validity of his self-evaluation. If the instigator exudes supreme confidence in his elevated self-evaluation, it is likely that the subject will think he is over-estimating his worth. Additionally, with respect to certain dimensions at least, there are quasi-objective clues as to his approximately correct valuation. In some situations, his use of language, the quickness of his response, and so on are usable as validating criteria. Finally, there are social clues from which a valid estimate of worth can be inferred. Important among these is the instigator's professional status. In some studies, instigators have been professors of psychology; in others, graduate students. Typically, these indicators are regarded as more valid than the instigator's self-evaluation.

Aggressive reactions which reflect an attempt to validate a social valuation are not the only possible reactions to boasting. A person who evaluates himself higher than his true worth in some respect may be found riotously funny or an object of sympathy by those who interact with him. Of course, mixed reactions can occur simultaneously or follow one another in quick succession. On a purely intuitive basis, the reaction of amusement seems to turn on the baselessness of the boast. If the self-evaluation is so exaggerated as to be beyond the realm of reality, it tends to become ridiculous and absurd. The laughter aroused by the proud butler, nose in the air, who trips and goes sprawling is an expression of the incongruous self-evaluation principle underlying much comedy. Sympathy arises from the perception that boasting has ruinous consequences for the individual who practices it. The sadness is enhanced when the individual is blind to the deleterious effects and must, by virtue of some ineradicable condition of character or situation, act out the tragic finale. Perhaps more than anyone else, Charlie Chaplin, with his plucky self-confidence, haughty air, and aristocratic pretense, was able to be both preposterous and sad at the same time.

For experimental purposes, the foregoing analysis suggests that the prediction of negative reactions to boastfulness depends on keeping the boasts within the borders of reality and without morbid consequences. A further requirement is that subjects believe in the sincerity of the person's boastfulness. If the other person is seen as an experimenter who is playing a role and testing their reactions, none of the above mentioned reactions can be expected. In other words, the boasting must occur as part of a natural interaction with the subject.

Apart from the way the boasting is carried out, the main problem in checking on a validation interpretation of negative evaluations is to make sure the subject is not threatened with a loss of status. One approach to this problem is to create a boastful but nonthreatening personality. For example, boasting can be made to reflect a vast self-interest and egomania rather than competitiveness. If the subject reacts negatively to such a harmless braggart, it is not likely that he is defending against a loss of status. There are additional implications which differentiate the status-threat and cognitive-validation interpretations of negative reactions shown toward a boastful person. A necessary condition for supposing the existence of a status threat is that the individual believes or thinks it is possible that he is inferior in those dimensions in which the boasting takes place. If he could reject the insinuation out of hand, there would be no need to defend himself. This means that the boaster's self-evaluation also must be believed or considered plausible, for without the invidious comparison, there would be no threat. The arousal of a cognitive-validation need, on the other hand, is based on the perception that the boaster's self-evaluation is invalid. But this distinction is difficult to measure directly. Although a subject under validation motivation would presumably make the judgment that the boaster is not as good as he thinks he is, the subject motivated by status threat would also make this judgment. Indeed, part of the pattern of his status-defensive behavior would be some form of denial that the boaster is as good as he claims.

However, there is an implication of the distinction which presumably can be measured. Status threat arises from a devaluation or attempted devaluation of the individual. One basic response to boastfulness which carries a status threat is an attempt to change or to resist the devaluation, not only by denying that the boaster is as good as he thinks he is, but by affirming that one's worth is not as low as is implicitly or explicitly alleged by the boaster. Thus, if motivated by status threat, the subject can be expected to make defensive self-evaluations. He should make himself out to be more attractive when interacting with a boaster than when interacting with more modest persons. On the other hand, when boastfulness generates a validation motive in the subject with respect to the boaster's valuation, the subject's self-evaluation is unaffected.

Secondly, in order for a status threat to be generated, the boaster must be sufficiently authoritative in his self-evaluation to make the subject entertain the possibility of his own inferiority. In such a situation, one might expect the subject to inhibit any overt expression of aggression. Specifically, if status threat underlies any of the aggressiveness in response to a boaster, one might expect a large discrepancy between the amount of aggression shown in public and the amount recorded in private. If the subject is motivated to validate a social valuation, on the other hand, the subject has no fear of being devalued, no perception of relatively greater power in the boaster, and, on these grounds, relatively little inhibition in the expression of hostile evaluations. Consequently, the public-private discrepancy in aggressiveness should be minimal or nonexistent.

Intervening theoretically between a status threat and its status-defensive responses is the emotional state of anger. According to a conceptualization discussed in Chapter 1, the level of anger is affected by the amount of aggression overtly expressed. If the so-called catharsis effect has any validity, it carries an implication which can help clarify the reaction to boastfulness.

Thus, if the aggressive behavior stimulated by boastfulness is motivated by status threat, then the more it is expressed overtly, the greater the quantity of anger drained off and the lower the subsequent aggressiveness. On the other hand, if aggressive behavior reflects a cognitive-validation process, no anger is involved. Consequently, no inverse relationship is predicted between the amount of aggressiveness openly expressed toward a boaster and the immediately subsequent amount of aggressiveness toward him.

A simple experimental procedure was devised which would enable us to see whether the boastfulness of another person does produce negative evaluations of him on the part of the subject and, in the light of the foregoing analysis, enable us to make an assessment of the cognitive-validation hypothesis.

PROCEDURE AND MEASURES

Subjects were undergraduate male students at the University of Pennsylvania. They were volunteers recruited for the announced purpose of participating in a survey dealing with student social activities. They came to the appointed room individually and were met by a first-year graduate student who introduced himself as an "assistant to the research director" who had been assigned to conduct the survey interview.

Each subject was assigned at random to the experimental or control condition. In the former, the interviewer expressed an extremely high self-evaluation and an extremely high degree of confidence in his self-evaluation.[1] His boasting was specifically based upon the remarks he interpolated among the standard interview questions and upon the manner in which these remarks were made. However, so that his boastfulness would be seen as a reflection of egocentricity rather than competitiveness, the interviewer's attitude and manner were impersonal and

1. The characterizations of the manner in which the interviewer made his self-augmenting remarks are reconstructions of his behavior as it appeared on several occasions to an observer. Many hours of training were required to bring the interviewer's performance to a fine point of skill.

clinically detached both in the posing of the questions and the
recording of the subject's responses. He carefully avoided focus
on the individual subject; he was fixed narcissistically upon himself. The questions asked, the interpolated remarks, and the
conduct of the interviewer in the experimental condition were
essentially as follows:
Arriving a few minutes late, the interviewer began the interview
by saying:

> I don't have much time. I'd like to get this over with
> —I have more important things to do.

Then he asked:

> Do you like Philadelphia?

Regardless of the answer, while recording it indifferently, he
said:

> I can hardly wait to leave this place and get back up
> to New York. Philadelphia is a pretty dull town.

He asked routinely:

> Do you date girls? How often during the week?

Then, obviously pleased with himself:

> Not a big social life—I used to date several times a
> week.

Returning to the interview, he asked:

> How many different girls do you date?

Whatever the answer, he was pleased with himself when he
pointed out:

> When I was your age, it was a different girl each time.

As if still in a reverie about his own past love life, he wondered:

> What do you do on a date? Dance? Go to the movies?
> Do you kiss your date goodnight the first time you've
> been out with her?

So that the subject should not make the mistake of underestimat-
ing him:

> I usually started an affair the first night.

Continuing in this narcissistic vein:

> Does your date enjoy your company? Do you consider
> yourself sexually adequate?

When asked about the meaning of sexual adequacy, he repeated the question and said:

It's what you think it means,

and with a smile of self-satisfaction:

I know what it means.

He then asked objectively:

How much do you usually spend on a date?

To reinforce his man-about-town image, he commented:

I would think nothing of dropping $50 or $60 in one evening.

The interview was concluded with a question about the subject's dress. To understand the massively self-oriented nature of the question, it is necessary to note that the interviewer was impeccably dressed in the Ivy style, with dark brown tweed jacket and charcoal gray trousers. He invariably puffed on an expensive briar and sported a junior-sized regimental mustache. As if looking at himself in the mirror, he asked rhetorically:

Do you always come to appointments dressed as you are now?

In the control condition, there were no interpolated remarks and no mannerisms designed to project the image of an inflated ego. The questions were exactly the same and the interviewer's attitude toward the subject in recording the responses was again clinically detached and indifferent.

There were two measures of the subject's evaluation of the interviewer and of himself. The first was taken "in public" in that the subject evaluated the interviewer in the latter's presence. Specifically, the subject was asked to free-associate about his feelings toward the interviewer in accordance with the following instructions:

Do you know what free association is? It is saying about yourself or some other person or any subject anything that comes to your mind without any restraint or inhibition whatsoever. Now I'd like you to sit, facing the wall, and begin to free-associate about me. Just say anything you want about me—anything goes—don't hold back.

After four minutes of free associations about the interviewer, the subject vocalized descriptions and evaluations of himself for the same amount of time.

Following the free-association procedure, each subject was given in private a set of personality-trait rating scales. There were eighteen positive scales including "adaptable," "capable," "cultured," "strong," and other obviously favorable traits of personality. The eighteen negative scales included "uncouth," "lazy," "pretentious," "dull," "insipid," and other unfavorable traits. Adjacent to each adjective was a 6-point rating scale, representing the degree of the positive or negative trait. It was emphasized that responses to these scales would be held strictly confidential. The interviewer said that he would not see the ratings until a later phase of the research program and then only in the form of grouped tabular data in which individual responses could not be identified. After the subject evaluated the interviewer on the scales, he evaluated himself using an identical instrument.

Following the private evaluations, the subjects were told that they had been in an experiment. A thorough explanation of the purposes and procedures of the study was given, and the subjects were dismissed with thanks.

The evaluations of the interviewer and other verbal material contained in the "public" free associations were readily grouped into four exhaustive categories: *Positive, Negative, Neutral,* and *Uncertain.* In the first two categories were clear-cut positive or negative evaluations of the interviewer and of the subject himself. For example:

> ... you have a pleasing personality....
> ... my outlook is cosmopolitan....
> I have good marks, on the basis of which I conclude I have a high IQ.

Coded as *Negative* evaluations were:

> You're probably not the kind of person I'd make a friend of.
>
> Don't know whether I'd like to drink with you and discuss past experiments.
>
> Sometimes I feel I don't fit into society; it worries me.
>
> I'm cold and unresponsive to many things and ideas.

In the *Neutral* category were nonevaluative statements, including descriptions of the weather, the room, clothing, and other physical objects. For example:

> It's warm in here.
> I wear glasses.
> I am six feet tall.

The *Uncertain* category included associations with an ambiguous or equivocal meaning. For example, a statement like "You're pretty tweedy" in reference to the interviewer could be a sartorial compliment or a derisive remark. By itself, such a statement does not allow a clear-cut decision.

To check on the reliability of coding according to this scheme, an independent judge went through all the statements, categorizing them in terms of the formally specified definitions. The two codings were in 89 per cent agreement.

PUBLIC EVALUATIONS

As shown in Table 1, subjects interviewed by the boaster openly expressed considerable aggression toward him. Specifically, there were more negative evaluations and fewer positive evaluations of him than of the nonboastful interviewer. In terms of the relative frequency of aggressive behaviors, indicated by parentheses, there were three times as many negative evaluations and about half as many positive evaluations of him as in the control condition. It is worth noting that the negative reactions included cutting criticism, sarcasm, and bold assertions of contempt. There were no differences between conditions in the mean number of *Neutral* and *Uncertain* statements. The table also makes clear that boasting had no effect on the subject's expressed self-evaluation.

TABLE 1
MEAN NUMBER OF OVERT ASSOCIATIONS TO
INTERVIEWER AND SELF

	Experimental Condition			
Evaluations	*Boastful* (N = 25)		*Nonboastful* (N = 25)	
	Interviewer	Self	Interviewer	Self
Positive	2.76*(34%)	7.64(62%)	6.52*(60%)	8.12(60%)
Negative	2.64†(33)	3.44(28)	1.08†(19)	3.36(25)
Neutral	1.60 (20)	.84(7)	1.88 (17)	1.00(7.5)
Uncertain	1.08 (13)	.32(3)	1.44 (13)	1.00(7.5)
	100	100	100	100

*t = 4.58, p < .01
†t = 2.40, p < .05

PRIVATE EVALUATIONS

The rating scales used to assess the private evaluation of the interviewer and of the subject himself were scored simply by adding the positive and negative personality ratings. Table 2 gives the mean evaluations of interviewer and subject under the experimental and control conditions.

TABLE 2
MEAN PERSONALITY RATINGS OF INTERVIEWER
AND SELF RECORDED PRIVATELY

	Experimental Condition		
Evaluation of Interviewer	*Boastful* (N = 25)	*Nonboastful* (N = 25)	
Positive	74.9	78.9	
Negative	49.1	41.8	t = 4.61, p < .01
Evaluation of Self			
Positive	73.4	74.8	
Negative	55.8	51.0	

The results resemble the pattern of evaluations expressed by the public free associations. Subjects who interacted with the boastful interviewer portray through their ratings a definitely more unattractive personality than those who have interacted with the more modest interviewer. The positive evaluation of the interviewer is also markedly lower, although not significantly so. As in the free-association material, there are no differences between conditions in the positive and negative self-evaluations reflected in the personality-trait ratings.

ASSESSMENT

There is little question that boastfulness brings forth a strong negative reaction under the conditions and with the sample of the present study. Apparently, the determinants of the other possible reactions to boastfulness discussed previously were sufficiently weak. The total pattern of findings also helps to distinguish between a status-threat and a cognitive-validation interpretation of the negative reaction.

As mentioned earlier, a threat to the individual's status can be assumed to arouse anger which then motivates status-defensive behavior. Assuming the validity of the catharsis hypothesis, if the overt negative evaluations of the boaster are reflections of anger, they should lower the amount of anger remaining in the subject. Such reduced anger, in turn, should make for less negative evaluations subsequently recorded in private.

A simple catharsis test of anger was made in the boastful condition, where there were strong and frequent negative evaluations expressed. The distribution of net positive evaluations of the interviewer—the number of positive minus the number of negative evaluations—expressed publicly by the subjects in the free-association procedure was drawn up and divided at the median into upper and lower halves. In the upper half were the subjects who expressed relatively few negative evaluations of the interviewer—a large frequency of net positive evaluations— whereas in the lower half were the subjects who released a relatively large amount of this form of aggression. Then, for each of these groups, the mean net positive evaluation of the interviewer, made in private following the free associations, was computed. Table 3 shows that there is no evidence of a cathartic reduction in anger; the mean evaluations of the boastful interviewer are very similar, and they bear no relation to the amount of hostility previously released by subjects.

TABLE 3
MEAN PERSONALITY RATINGS OF INTERVIEWER AS A FUNCTION OF PRIOR NEGATIVE OVERT ASSOCIATIONS

Overt Associations to Interviewer

	Relatively Negative* (N = 13)	Relatively Positive† (N = 12)
Personality Rating of Interviewer‡	21.3	27.7

*A low frequency of net positive (positive minus negative) associations.
†A high frequency of net positive (positive minus negative) associations.
‡The mean net positive (positive minus negative) personality-trait rating.

Tables 1 and 2 show clearly that, in terms of both free associations and rating scales, the boastful interviewer generated a relatively large amount of aggressive behavior. There is no evidence of inhibition in the public expression of negative attitudes. Consequently, the view that the status-threatening interviewer suppressed the overt expression of aggression is not supported. It also does not help the status-threat interpretation to note that neither public nor private self-evaluations were affected by the interviewer's boastfulness. That is, there is no sign whatever of defensive self-evaluations.

Although the results are thus thoroughly consistent with a validation interpretation, there is no definitive evidence in its support. When all is said and done, at least part of the negative attitudes toward the boastful interviewer could have been due to his egregious breach of good taste. To eliminate such an interpretive possibility and to support the cognitive-validation hypothesis, an experiment was needed in which the amount of boasting was held constant, while the criterion representing the person's true valuation was systematically varied. Such an experiment is discussed in the following chapter.

5 Attraction and Legitimate Conceit

In the exploratory experiment reported in the preceding chapter, the discrepancy between the interviewer's self-evaluation and some indication of his true valuation was not varied. It was not possible, therefore, to draw direct conclusions about the effects of an invalid estimate of another person's valuation. There were other deficiencies in that preliminary study. For example, although a determined attempt was made to create an egocentric, narcissistic, but nonthreatening person, some subjects may have felt that the interviewer was contemptuous and arrogant. Thus, it is possible that some subjects disliked this type of personality as such or were threatened in some way. To rule out such interpretations, it is necessary to eliminate or to hold constant the contemptuousness and any insinuation that the subject is inferior. In the ideal situation, the subject must not even be touched by threats which are implicit in his being invidiously compared. A further improvement would be to make the boasting less blatant so that it is less likely to be considered a breach of manners and taste.

In a study incorporating these recommended features, the subject was placed in a situation where he observed and evaluated a person whose self-evaluation, expressed in interaction with another party, was more or less excessive. The subject was not directly involved in the interaction; he was given a transcript of what he thought had been a real interaction between two persons. To vary the boastful person's apparent objective worth, his professional status was described to the subject as high or low. In all conditions of the experiment, the second person in the purportedly real interaction was a student. The hypothesis tested was: *The larger the discrepancy between a person's expressed opinion of himself and his apparent objective valuation, as approximately reflected by his professional status, the more negative the subject's evaluation of him.*

PROCEDURE AND MEASURES

Several undergraduate classes were used to provide a large number of subjects at the same time. The announced purpose of the study was to discover how people form impressions of others' personalities.

> Psychological studies have shown that people can fully describe another's character on the basis of very limited information. In everyday life, for example, letters, works of art, brief conversations, or mere social introductions sometimes result in remarkably comprehensive impressions of another person. Moreover, these first impressions are usually very lasting and often quite accurate. The purpose of this study is to contribute toward a better understanding of this process.

Following these general instructions, more specific material, designed to foster the subject's interest in the characters and situation, was given.

Try to imagine yourself a student eating lunch at the same table with the two discussants. William Jones is a student like yourself; Robert Brown is a. . . . *(Brown's status was indicated here and will be described below.)* The transcript you have is an excerpt of the actual conversation that took place between them concerning economic aid to an underdeveloped country, recorded exactly the way it occurred:

JONES: I'm completely ignorant about the problem. I hardly know what could be involved in the question of sending industrial equipment to Liberia. Maybe the temperature would have something to do with it. If the temperature is always too high, the Liberians wouldn't be able to work in factories.

BROWN: That's a point. One of the first crucial factors is the level of the technical skill which now exists among the natives or can be taught to them in a reasonable period of time. Using Dugway's revised ratio of manpower flexibility, I would say that the ratio of skilled workers in Liberia must be at least above the fortieth percentile to make a large industrial expansion feasible.

JONES: Maybe we ought also to consider whether or not the Liberians want the machines. Maybe they would be more content without them. We could do an opinion survey to find out.

BROWN: It's a possibility. Besides the level of technical skill, we must examine Claude Metraux's Index of Economic Geography, and of course Julian Weinert's *Exportation Handbook,* to determine the amount of Liberia's potential market being met by other countries. If there are friendly powers who would be adversely affected, then our policy must take that into consideration.

JONES: Maybe if we determined that the soil, rainfall weren't good for farm equipment, this would mean that the U.S. should send them industrial equipment. We obviously wouldn't want to waste the farm equipment.

BROWN: There's something to what you say. Finally, the analysis must also include the availability of potential power resources, without which the rate of expansion and profit would be negligible. This factor can easily be determined since, by summing the known BTU's of coal resources with a weighted index of oil and potential water power, a figure can be obtained which correlates highly with the log of the rate of maximum feasible expansion of industry.

Brown's comments were carefully designed to give subjects the impression that he thought rather highly of himself. In a preliminary survey, several independent judges agreed that such an effect was achieved. He is not only supremely confident of his views, which he presented with a rapid-fire assurance, but, in his high-flown technical analysis, he exhibits an absorbing egocentricity.

According to the hypothesis, the reaction to Brown's self-defined superiority will depend upon how valid it is. Its validity, in turn, is assumed to be determined by Brown's professional status in a field relevant to the dimension in which the superior attitude is expressed. Variations in his professional-status position were created specifically as follows:

In the *Low-Status* condition (created just prior to the subject's reading of the dialogue), Brown was introduced as a student, an undergraduate like Jones. In the *High-Status* condition, Brown was introduced as an important official.

Dr. Brown is a high official in the State Department's African Plans and Program Division.

In what may be termed a *Super-Status* condition, Brown is described as a world-renowned expert.

Dr. Brown occupies the R. H. Van Heusen chair of Political Science at Harvard. He is a highly paid consultant to the State Department's African Plans and Program Division and is the acknowledged authority in the field. By his colleagues the world over, he is considered to be one of the finest minds of the generation.

The subject's evaluations of Brown and Jones were obtained by two different kinds of instruments: 1) an 8-point rating scale, ranging from "dislike him intensely" on the low end, to "like him very much" on the high, and 2) an open-ended question which requested the subject to describe in detail his feelings about the discussants.

VALIDITY OF BROWN'S ABILITY

The first consideration is whether a discrepancy between the estimate of his own worth which Brown conveyed and his professional status did vary in size across the experimental conditions, as was intended. Specifically, did subjects regard the validity of Brown's highly positive self-attitude as dependent upon his professional status? Data on the perceived validity of Brown's self-estimation were obtained through a content analysis of the subject's feelings toward him in response to the open-ended question. First, the subjects who made an explicit judgment about Brown's ability were selected from the entire combined sample of subjects. Then, of those who did make such a judgment, a tabulation was made of the number who questioned or doubted Brown's ability and the number who acknowledged it. The coding of each subject's response into one of three categories—*Ability Doubted, Ability Acknowledged, Ability Not Mentioned*—was accomplished, of course, without knowledge of the experimental condition from which the subject was drawn. The following quotations help define the categories in the cases where an ability evaluation was made.

Brown's Ability Doubted

Seems to be a guy who likes to talk but doesn't know much.

I think Brown is a phony intellectual type who

probably doesn't know what he's talking about but
tries to impress people.

... a know-it-all, but not really.

Brown's Ability Acknowledged

Dr. Brown seems to be a man who knows fairly
well what he is talking about.

... is a very capable, intelligent, rational person.

... a man well versed in his field.

An independent coding of a 50 per cent sample of cases into
all categories attained an agreement of 85 per cent with the original coding.

TABLE 4

PERCENTAGE OF SUBJECTS WHO DOUBT OR ACKNOWLEDGE
BROWN'S ABILITY ACCORDING TO HIS PROFESSIONAL STATUS

Brown's Professional Status	Ability Doubted	Ability Acknowledged	No Mention of Ability	
Low (N = 50)	66	16	18	100
High (N = 45)	60	27	13	100
Super (N = 44)*	41	39	20	100

χ^2 Over-all (4 df) = 8.27, p < .09
χ^2 Doubt vs. other (2 df) = 6.41, p < .05

* One subject did not respond

It is clear that, as Brown's status gets lower, the relative
frequency of subjects who doubt his ability goes up, and the
number of subjects who acknowledge his ability goes down. The
difference in frequency between the "doubters" and the other
categories across status conditions is a strong and significant one.
The degree to which Brown's expressed self-assessment exceeded
his true value did, in fact, vary across the experimental conditions, as intended. Accordingly, we may assume that the hypothetical need for validation was operating to a degree dependent

on the discrepancy between Brown's self-estimate and his professional status.

QUANTITATIVE EVALUATIONS

We now turn to the major experimental issue—the question of how Brown's attractiveness varies with the discrepancy between his highly positive self-evaluation and his professional status. Table 5 contains the mean attractiveness ratings of Brown and Jones. Recalling that it was an 8-unit scale, it appears that the average evaluations of Brown are not enthusiastic. Only the Brown who has *Super Status* gets an average rating that is on the "like" side of the scale, and just barely so. As for the effect of professional status, when Brown has *Super Status,* he is disliked significantly less than the Brown who has *Low Status,* with the mean rating of the *High-Status* Brown falling in between. The evidence is thus consistent with the hypothesis: Brown is negatively evaluated to the extent that his self-evaluation exceeds his true worth, as represented by his professional status.

TABLE 5

MEAN ATTRACTIVENESS RATINGS OF BROWN AND JONES: BROWN HAS HIGH SELF-EVALUATION AND VARYING STATUS

	Attractiveness	
Brown's Status	*Brown*	*Jones*
Low	4.32	6.79
$(N = 50)$		
High	4.71	5.57
$(N = 45)$		
Super	5.02	5.63
$(N = 45)$		
	$F = 3.11, p < .05$	$F = 7.54, p < .001$

Pairwise comparisons of status conditions by t-tests, employing within-group variance estimate with 138 df.

Brown		*Jones*	
Low vs. Super	$t = 2.50, p < .01$	Low vs. Super	$t = 4.14, p < .001$
Low vs. High	NS*	Low vs. High	$t = 4.35, p < .001$
High vs. Super	NS	High vs. Super	NS

* Not significant.

The picture with respect to the evalution of Jones is exactly the reverse. Although Jones' behavior is absolutely constant in all three conditions, how much he is liked depends upon how much Brown is liked (or upon the incorrectness of Brown's self-evaluation). Jones is most liked when Brown is evaluated most negatively, that is, when his self-estimate theoretically is most invalid. Jones is liked least when the dislike of Brown is at a minimum, that is, when Brown's superior self-evaluation is closest to being correct. As far as the averages are concerned, then, there appears to be a contrast effect in the evaluations of Jones. It is possible that the evaluation of Jones is determined by the validity of Brown's self-estimate in addition to being determined by direct contrast with the attractiveness of Brown. In other words, when Brown grossly overvalues himself, Jones tends to be perceived as selling himself short. The positive evaluation of Jones to some extent may reflect a validation process in which his apparent undervaluation is rejected. It is also possible that, instead of validating their evaluations of Brown directly, some subjects validate their evaluations of Jones in contrast to their evaluations of Brown.

QUALITATIVE EVALUATIONS

A simple content analysis of the open-ended material gives essentially the same picture as the quantitative ratings. Three categories were established after examining a subsample of the data. A coding was then made without identifying the experimental conditions. A statement about either of the discussants which was a wholly or predominantly positive evaluation was scored +1. For example:

> His [Brown's] abilities to dig deep into the facts to cover all the various points of a policy show his degree of reliability in his occupation.
> A likable individual and a leader of his class.

Statements devoid of evaluation were scored 0. Negative opinions about either of the discussants were scored −1. Examples of the latter are:

> Somewhat slow, not too capable . . . doesn't consider when he talks.
>
> Jones seems to be a rather dull person, and I find my feeling passive toward him.

A second coding by an independent judge resulted in an agreement of slightly over 80 per cent with respect to the assignment of the entire sample to the three categories.

Table 6 shows the mean qualitative attractiveness scores of

TABLE 6

MEAN QUALITATIVE ATTRACTION SCORES OF BROWN AND JONES: BROWN HAS HIGH SELF-EVALUATION AND VARYING STATUS[1]

	Attractiveness	
Brown's Status	*Brown*	*Jones*
Low	−.74	+.68
(N = 50)		
High	−.62	+.29
(N = 45)		
Super	−.36	+.11
(N = 44)*		
	F = 2.83, p < .07	F = 10.29, p < .001

Pairwise comparisons of status conditions are made by t-tests, employing within-group variance estimates with 137 df.

Brown		*Jones*	
Low vs. Super	t = 2.38, p < .02	Low vs. Super	t = 3.56, p < .01
Low vs. High	NS	Low vs. High	t = 2.43, p < .02
High vs. Super	NS	High vs. Super	NS

* One subject did not respond.

1. With such a qualitative measure, the assumptions underlying a parametric statistical test may not have been met. Consequently, the hypothesis of a chance frequency distribution of subjects who make either positive or negative evaluations of Brown and Jones was tested by chi square (2 df), employing marginal totals to compute theoretical frequencies.

Brown: $\chi^2 = 7.49$, p < .03
Jones: $\chi^2 = 9.96$, p < .01

Inspection of these distributions, which significantly depart from chance, reveals that, in the case of Brown, as his status goes down, the proportion of subjects who negatively evaluate him goes up. With Jones, it is the opposite. The more incorrect Brown is in his self-evaluation, the greater the proportion of subjects who positively evaluate Jones.

Brown and Jones under the three levels of Brown's professional status. As in the preceding quantitative ratings, Brown is not especially attractive, but he is disliked most when he has *Low Status* and disliked least when he has *Super Status*. The *High-Status* Brown is evaluated in between the significantly different extreme status positions.

The evaluation of Jones is definitely more positive. Moreover, compared with Brown, the trend of averages is reversed. He is most liked when Brown is most disliked and most disliked when Brown is most liked, that is, when Brown's self-estimate requires minimal validating.

STATUS IDENTIFICATION

Although the results are in line with the hypothesis, an alternative interpretation needs to be considered. Simply stated, it is possible that subjects admired Brown's status position as such. Even though the experiment was designed so that subjects could not directly be affected by Brown's behavior, his status position may have been admired by them. Such admiration may be based upon the vicarious achievement of power and prestige, the fantasy of being admired, and so forth. Whatever the basis, the attitude toward status in its own right could explain the results.

A partial solution of this interpretive problem consists in showing that Brown's status position is not the exclusive determinant of the subject's evaluation of him. If, in other words, with Brown's status position constant, the evaluation of him still varies with how positively Brown evaluates himself—that is, varies with how much Brown's self-evaluation departs from the true valuation inferred from his professional status—then clearly it is not status identification or admiration alone which explains the subject's evaluation of him.

Two additional experimental conditions were, therefore, established. In each, Brown's behavior implied a less extremely positive self-evaluation than in the original condition. In both conditions, Brown was given low status—that is, he was a student. The behavior of Jones, the student, was, of course, exactly the same as in the original conditions. Specifically, in the *Moderate* condition, Brown expressed a medium positive self-evaluation by the following remarks:

> JONES: . . . If the temperature is always too high, the Liberians wouldn't be able to work in factories.
>
> BROWN: That's a point. A possible factor might be the number of workers available to work in the factories. If there weren't enough workers, there wouldn't be enough people to run the machines and that wouldn't be too good.
>
> JONES . . . Maybe the Liberians don't want the machines. . . . We could do an opinion survey to find out.
>
> BROWN: It's a possibility. It might be important to find out if some other country who is friendly to the U.S. would get sore at giving them industrial equipment. Maybe they wouldn't buy any of Liberia's products.
>
> JONES: . . . We obviously wouldn't want to waste . . . farm equipment.
>
> BROWN: There's something to what you say. Offhand, I think we might also consider whether or not they have enough trees and coal to burn . . . to run the machinery. If they didn't, I'll bet it would cost a lot to bring it into the country.

Compared with the original dialogue, Brown has a less exaggerated opinion of himself. He still seems to think he is a superior person and gives the impression of self-interest. But his analysis is less high flown, he sounds a bit less certain, and he appears to have only slightly more knowledge on the issue than Jones does. The second experimental condition, *Low* self-evaluation, was one in which Brown expresses a self-evaluation slightly lower than in the *Moderate* condition. Jones's contributions to the discussion are the same as always.

> JONES: . . . if the temperature is always too high, the Liberians wouldn't be able to work in factories.

BROWN: In addition to temperature, a possible factor might be the number of workers available to work in the factories. If there weren't enough workers, there wouldn't be enough people to run the machines and that would make for difficulties.

JONES: Maybe the Liberians don't want the machines. . . . We could do an opinion survey to find out.

BROWN: Along that line, it might be important to find out if some other country which is friendly to the U.S. would get sore at giving them industrial equipment. Maybe they wouldn't buy any of Liberia's products.

JONES: . . . We obviously wouldn't want to waste . . . farm equipment.

BROWN: Offhand, I think we might also consider whether or not they have enough natural resources like coal and trees to burn . . . to run the machinery. If they didn't have enough, I'll bet it would cost a lot to bring it into the country.

In this role, Brown definitely appears more modest in his implied self-appraisal. The phrases which reflect self-evaluation in the *Moderate* condition, like "That's a point" and "It's a possibility," have been eliminated. According to several pretests, the over-all effect is that Brown now evaluates himself at about the same level that Jones does.

Table 7 shows the average attractiveness of the two discussants. Looking at Brown, it is evident that, although his status is constant, the evaluations of him vary according to his expressed self-evaluation. As his expression of superiority decreases, subjects evaluate him less negatively. In terms of the scale descriptions, when he expresses an extremely high self-estimate (the original condition), he is "disliked a little"; when his self-evaluation is low, he is actually "liked a little." The attractiveness of the *Moderate* Brown lies in between the *High* and *Low*. The difference between *High* and *Low*, as well as between *Moderate* and *Low*, is statistically significant.

TABLE 7

MEAN ATTRACTIVENESS RATINGS OF BROWN AND JONES: BROWN
HAS LOW STATUS AND VARYING SELF-EVALUATION

	Attractiveness	
Brown's Self-Evaluation	*Brown*	*Jones*
High	4.32	6.79
(N = 50)		
Moderate	4.45	5.07
(N = 45)*		
Low	5.26	4.90
(N = 43)†		

$F = 6.62$, $p < .005$ $F = 28.8$, $p < .001$

Pairwise comparisons of experimental conditions by t-tests, employing
within-group variance estimates with 136 df.

Brown		*Jones*	
High vs. Low	$t = 3.48$, $p < .01$	High vs. Low	$t = 7.00$, $p < .001$
High vs. Moderate	NS	High vs. Moderate	$t = 6.37$, $p < .001$
Moderate vs. Low	$t = 2.89$, $p < .01$	Moderate vs. Low	NS

* Two subjects did not make rating.
† One subject did not make rating.

The average liking of Jones, whose behavior was constant,
again runs in the opposite direction, indicating a cognitive
contrast effect. He is most liked—almost "strongly"—when
Brown is most disliked; he is least liked—"a little"—when
Brown's self-evaluation is modest.

As far as the quantitative ratings are concerned, we can say
that the attractiveness of Brown, when he expresses a self-evaluation which is higher than his apparent objective status would
seem to warrant, is *not* exclusively due to the subject's attitude
toward his status as such.

The qualitative evaluations of Brown and Jones based on
the open-ended verbal material are perfectly consistent with the
ratings. As shown in Table 8, with Brown's status constant as
a student, his attractiveness depends upon how extreme his self-
evaluation is. The more he seems to think of himself, the more
negatively he is evaluated. The evaluation of Jones, whose ex-

pressed self-evaluation and behavior in general is entirely constant, is also affected by Brown's self-evaluation, but in the reverse direction. Jones is liked most when Brown's self-evaluation is most excessive; he is liked least when Brown is most modest in his self-evaluation.

TABLE 8

MEAN QUALITATIVE ATTRACTION SCORES OF BROWN AND JONES: BROWN HAS LOW STATUS AND VARYING SELF-EVALUATION[2]

	Attractiveness	
Brown's Self-Evaluation	*Brown*	*Jones*
High	−.74	+.68
(N = 50)		
Moderate	−.32	−.09
(N = 47)		
Low	−.18	−.29
(N = 44)		

$F = 6.74, p < .005$ $F = 18.24, p < .001$

Pairwise comparisons of experimental conditions by t-tests, employing within-group variance estimates with 139 df.

Brown		*Jones*	
High vs. Low	$t = 3.50, p < .005$	High vs. Low	$t = 5.70, p < .001$
High vs. Moderate	$t = 2.37, p < .02$	High vs. Moderate	$t = 4.53, p < .001$
Moderate vs. Low	NS	Moderate vs. Low	NS

2. Again, because these qualitative measures may involve impermissible assumptions for a parametric test of differences in means, the hypothesis was tested that the distribution of subjects who evaluate the discussants either positively or negatively across the three experimental conditions is a chance distribution. Using the marginal totals to generate the theoretical frequencies, chi squares 2 df are:

Brown: $\chi^2 = 10.16, p < .01$
Jones: $\chi^2 = 28.64, p < .001$

Inspection shows that, as Brown's self-evaluation becomes more extremely positive, the number of subjects who negatively evaluate him in their open-ended comments increases. With Jones, the opposite is true.

In these experiments, we chose to hold Brown's status constant at the lowest level in order to maximize the possibility that his expressed self-evaluation would be perceived as excessive. Although the interpretation seems clear enough, one could claim that the attitude toward status as such was weak or nonexistent at this level. Perhaps, if Brown's status were held constant at a higher level, one would find that positive attitudes toward it are so strong that differences in the degree of Brown's expressed superiority would not result in corresponding "corrective" evaluations of him. Such a result would suggest that the hypothesized validation process only determines the evaluations of other persons when other determinants, such as the status of such persons, are of a low order of magnitude or are absent altogether. These considerations led to the design of still another study in which Brown was, as in the original condition, a high official in the State Department—*High Status*—but in which he expressed a moderate self-evaluation. His attractiveness to subjects under these conditions could then be compared with his attractiveness under one of the original conditions in which he had the same high status, but where he expressed a high self-evaluation.

TABLE 9

MEAN ATTRACTIVENESS RATINGS OF BROWN AND JONES: BROWN
HAS HIGH STATUS AND VARYING SELF-EVALUATION

	Attractiveness	
Brown's Self-Evaluation	*Brown*	*Jones*
High	4.71	5.57
(N = 45)		
Moderate	4.69	4.97
(N = 47)*		
		t = 1.93, p < .06

* One subject did not make rating.

Table 9 shows that, as far as the quantitative ratings are concerned, the attractiveness of Brown is not affected by the variation in his self-evaluation. The evaluation of Jones, whose behavior was constant, is more favorable, however, when Brown expresses a very superior self-evaluation.

Table 10 reports on the qualitative evaluations of Brown. With high status constant, it can be seen that he is more disliked when he expresses a high self-evaluation. As usual, Jones is evaluated more positively when Brown is most unattractive and

evaluated somewhat, though not significantly, less positively
when Brown is moderate in his self-evaluation.

TABLE 10

MEAN QUALITATIVE ATTRACTION SCORES OF BROWN AND JONES:
BROWN HAS HIGH STATUS AND VARYING SELF-EVALUATION

Brown's Self-Evaluation	Attractiveness	
	Brown	Jones
High	−.62	+.29
(N = 45)		
Moderate	−.29	+.08
(N = 48)		

t = 1.89, p < .06

ASSESSMENT

The experiments tested the hypothesis that evaluations of
another person depend upon the discrepancy between the person's expressed self-evaluation and his professional status. The
postulated need of the individual to maintain a valid cognitive
structure with respect to the valuation of relevant others in his
social environment appears to handle the findings quite well.
When the expressed self-evaluation of a person is higher than
the true level which the subject infers from the person's professional status, the subject tends to evaluate him negatively. The
rejection of an invalid estimate of another's valuation and the
acceptance of a relatively correct estimate appear to reflect an
underlying cognitive-validation process. It should be noted that
the evaluations of Brown were recorded in absolute privacy and
under the strictest conditions of anonymity. The evaluations
were made when the subject was not in a face-to-face relation
with Brown and, thus, could neither be inhibited nor threatened
by the latter's behavior or status. It would seem very unlikely,
therefore, that subjects could have been angered and reacted
negatively in order to defend against a status loss.

An alternative interpretation was considered: The evaluation of Brown could have been based entirely upon the latter's
status. Experiments were designed to eliminate this possibility.

Status was held constant at a low level, while self-evaluation was made to vary from very modest through moderate to extremely high. In another study, status was held constant at a high level with the self-evaluation high or moderate. The evidence was fairly clear that Brown's attractiveness depended upon how highly he evaluated himself—and, theoretically, upon the extent to which the valuation was warranted.

It is still possible, of course, that Brown's status position was a *partial* determinant of his attractiveness. Thus, when Brown's self-evaluation was held constant, the positive attitude which subjects held toward status could have determined his attractiveness. It could also be claimed that negative attitudes toward conceit had a partial effect. That is, when Brown's status was held constant, the hostility toward him could have depended upon the degree of conceit he displayed. Conceivably, then, there might have been two independent effects involved in the reaction to Brown, rather than the hypothesized single effect based upon the validity of his self-evaluation. Such an interpretive possibility is clearly admissible and will have to be dealt with. However, what makes it less compelling is the evidence that the frequency of explicit doubt concerning Brown's ability varied across experimental conditions inversely with his attractiveness. The coincidence of attractiveness and the experimentally created discrepancy between Brown's self-evaluation and professional status lends more support to the validation hypothesis than to the status-admiration interpretation. The other aspect of the admissible alternative is that a negative attitude toward conceit would not easily explain the relatively low attractiveness of Brown when he expressed a moderate self-evaluation.

6 Valid Boastfulness and Invalid Self-Depreciation

The reaction to exaggerated self-importance has been interpreted in part as the reflection of a validation process in which an individual forms an evaluation of another person which corresponds to what he defines as the valid or true worth of that person. Thus, when the individual's estimate of another person's worth is lower, according to a dependable criterion of validity, than that person's self-estimate, the person is evaluated negatively. Theoretically, this process should be symmetrical. That is, using the same criterion of validity, if the true worth of the person is *higher* than that person's self-estimate, he should be *positively* evaluated, reflecting the rejection of the invalid self-estimate. An experiment was designed to check this implication of the validation hypothesis. In addition, so that the validation process can be demonstrated in both positive and negative directions under the same over-all conditions, a companion experiment was also run involving a self-overestimation on the part of a "stimulus" person. Employing professional status to represent a valid estimate of a person's worth in a certain sphere, two hypotheses were tested:

> 1. A boastful person who has high professional status will be evaluated less negatively than a boastful person of low status.
>
> 2. A self-depreciating person who has high professional status will be evaluated more positively than a self-depreciating person of low status.

In the experiment involving a person who overestimated his capabilities, it was again necessary to eliminate the possibility that the subject would be threatened by being invidiously compared with such a person. First, although a real situation for the subject, the study was designed so that he was never in direct contact with the boastful person. Subjects were anonymous members of small groups and did not interact with the boastful interviewer at all. Second, the occasion calling for the subject's evaluation of the interviewer was an entirely different study, conducted in a different language, at a different time, in the absence of the interviewer. Thus, even if there had been a status threat generated by an indirect relationship with the boastful person, it is unlikely that it was operating at the time the evaluations were recorded.

PROCEDURE AND MEASURES

The experiments were carried out in the Netherlands, employing groups of Dutch university students as subjects. The groups were composed of subjects selected at random from a large pool of volunteers who had been recruited to participate in unspecified social-psychology studies. Groups of eight to ten subjects were assembled in a classroom and told that there would be two studies, one after the other, which were sponsored by a recognized intercultural organization (actually fictitious) with interests in cross-cultural research on university student life. The first study was to be a comprehensive survey of Dutch student life; the second, independent study, an investigation of impressions of personality.

The first study was described as a combination interview and group discussion. The English translation of the essential part of this orientation announcement is as follows:

> The research program in which you will participate is under the auspices of the Holland-U.S. Institute. The studies are concerned with different aspects of intercultural relations. Specifically, we have asked you here to participate in two short research projects. In the first, you'll be asked questions on your attitude toward a number of aspects of student life in the Netherlands. After that, you'll be asked to supply other information.
>
> And now for the first study. As we mentioned before, this is not a typical interview, but is a procedure between a personal interview and an opinion poll. One of you will be asked a few questions. Those of you not being questioned can listen to the respondent and think about the answers you would give. After the questioning, there will be short discussions about the issues concerned with Dutch student life. The interview will be conducted in English which will not present you with any difficulties.[1]

Certain control features of the design may be noted. In order to obtain subject evaluations of the interviewer which would not be influenced by the interviewer's punitive power or affected by threats of humiliation or any possibility of retaliation, the evaluations were made in the context of a second study with which the interviewer was to have no material connection. Although sponsored by the same organization concerned with intercultural relations, the two studies were said to be carried out by two

1. Dutch university students can speak or understand English at least moderately well.

different directors and focused on entirely different problems; they were also conducted in different languages. It should be kept in mind, too, that subjects were assured of complete privacy and anonymity in their answers.

Following the orientation announcement, the status variable was introduced as follows:

> *High Status:* The professor who directs the survey is the director of the Institute for Anthropological Research of Yale University and currently president of the United States Anthropological Association. He has earned a world-wide reputation from his studies on academic and intellectual elites and student life in a number of contemporary cultures. The Holland-U.S. Institute has requested him to direct this research, and he has agreed despite his very active professional life. The Institute considers his acceptance a great honor.
>
> *Low Status:* The man who will conduct the survey comes from Philadelphia, where he is a night-school student.
>
> He is attempting to write a dissertation for his doctoral degree concerning some aspects of student life. He learned that the Holland-U.S. Institute was taking the initiative in a number of studies on student life in different cultures, and he requested to take part. At first, it was not possible since all the places were taken, but, as luck would have it, the Institute was able to create one more. You can imagine his joy when the good news was received that he could take part.

About five minutes after the interview began, at a standard point in the questioning, the phone rang and was taken by the assistant. After ascertaining that the party could not call back, the assistant delivered the following message half-aloud to the interviewer:

> There is a call for you. It is long distance from
> Copenhagen. He says he can only call now—he has
> to catch a train.

The interviewer, surprised at the interruption, guessed who the
caller might be and the possible importance of the call. He said:

> I shall have to take this call now. Can I take it in
> the next room? This will take about twenty minutes,
> so I'm afraid this interview session is over. Perhaps
> I can finish with this group another day. You might
> use them now for your own study.

The interviewer then exited and the assistant said in the Dutch
language:

> As you can gather, [the interviewer] has had to
> terminate this interview. Perhaps he will bring you
> back for an individual interview some other time. But
> right now I can start the second study for which you
> are here. The study I am directing is concerned with
> the way people form impressions of others. It is joined
> to the first study because all of you have just been con-
> fronted with the same person. We are interested in
> the way Dutch students look at the various non-
> Dutchmen who conduct these studies for the Institute.
> So, on the lined paper that we are now passing out,
> we'd like you to jot down in short phrases and words
> just what you think of him, how you feel about him,
> and what your reaction is to him. I assure you that
> what you say will never be seen by him; you are com-
> pletely anonymous.

Subjects were given five minutes for these spontaneous evaluations of the interviewer. Two quantitative measures were then
distributed. One, a rating of the interviewer's professional status;
the second, a rating of the interviewer's attractiveness as a person.
Following these measures, the experiment was concluded. Subjects were given a complete explanation of the purposes and

procedures used and were requested to refrain from talking about the study for three weeks.

In all the studies of this series, the respondent, apparently chosen because he was the occupant of the first seat in the first row, had actually been a confederate. The different experimental conditions involving self-depreciation and boastfulness were created by way of the interviewer's interpolated remarks. In all conditions, of course, the interviewer was the same person. The actual questions and remarks designed to establish a *High Self-Evaluation* (boastfulness) or a *Low Self-Evaluation* (self-depreciation) condition were as follows:

INTERVIEWER: There are just a few questions for the student I interview. These are in different categories regarding student life. While I interview one person, the rest of you can prepare for the group discussion afterwards. The interview will be recorded on tape, so please speak up. I shall conduct the interview in English—don't worry about how good your English is.

(then)

(*High Self-Evaluation*) By the way, regarding languages, I have something of a talent—at least in the Romance and Slavic tongues. I speak French, Italian, and Spanish fluently, as well as Czech. I also do well in Hungarian.

(or)

(*Low Self-Evaluation*) By the way, regarding languages, my own ability at learning any foreign language is rather poor, I think. When I try to speak another language, it sounds pretty poor.

(then)

First, let's get some information about how much and how far Dutch students travel. After all, travel is a major source of intercultural education. During the year 1960, how many times have you traveled out of this country, and where?

STUDENT: Let's see . . . three times. Yes, once to Germany, once to Belgium, and a holiday to France last summer.

INTERVIEWER:

(*High Self-Evaluation*) I'm quite a world traveler, you know. I've been just about everywhere in Europe within the last six months. In fact, every free weekend I have, I try to spend in a different European capital.

(*or*)

(*Low Self-Evaluation*) My traveling is next to nothing. I hardly move out of my own city even when I have the opportunity.

(*then*)

Let's move on to the intellectual life of students—specifically books and reading. How many books do you have in your room at the present time—not school books, but biographies, novels, and so forth? About how many—an exact number is not necessary.

STUDENT: I just finished a book by De Mann and recently one by De Hartog . . . and a couple of other Dutch writers.

INTERVIEWER:

(*High Self-Evaluation*) I'm a voracious reader of novels. I'm extremely fond of subtle social situations which some novelists are able to develop.

(*or*)

(*Low Self-Evaluation*) Unfortunately, I've read very little of the really great world literature.

(*then*)

I have here the standard international student reading list. According to this survey, five authors have been read most often by students in the countries investigated. Which of the following classic authors on the list have you read: Mark Twain, Tolstoi, Dickens, Victor Hugo, Thomas Mann? Have you read any of these authors before or since coming to the university?

STUDENT: I've read Tolstoi—*War and Peace*—but not the others.

INTERVIEWER:

(High Self-Evaluation) Of course I read most of these authors' works—even the less popular ones—when I was still in high school.

(or)

(Low Self-Evaluation) One day I ought to read one of the works of these authors.

(then)

I'd now like to ask you a question about your field of study and how you look at it. What field are you preparing for—what are you studying?

STUDENT: Sociology (physics).[2]

INTERVIEWER: We have in this manual standard questions for each field. The question for sociology is: Which do you think is more important to society, sociology as studied in universities or practical social work (theoretical or applied physics)?

STUDENT: That is difficult to answer—in the long run, academic sociology (physics) is important, but applied social work (applied physics) also helps society.

INTERVIEWER:

(High Self-Evaluation) My own view is that there is a subtle interdependence between the theoretical and the applied social (physical) sciences. I've already impressed government officials with this view.

(or)

(Low Self-Evaluation) These complicated issues get me confused very easily.

2. The confederate who was interviewed in two sessions was a physics major. He mentioned his true specialty to allay the suspicion of any subject who might have been able to identify him on this basis. Before each session began, the confederates scanned the group and were unable to spot any subjects who knew them more than merely by sight. The confederates were, of course, originally chosen with this in mind.

(then)

About your life as a student—how many hours a week do you study?

STUDENT: A few hours each day—perhaps 20 hours a week.

INTERVIEWER:

(High Self-Evaluation) I am and always have been a great worker. I would think nothing of working 30 hours straight without sleep. Some people are born with a zest for work.

(or)

(Low Self-Evaluation) I never could study much and was never much of a student.

(then)

On the whole, what do you think of the professors here at the university?

STUDENT: Well—I think those I've had are very good.

INTERVIEWER:

(High Self-Evaluation) My own attitude toward professors can be looked upon as a model. I respected some very much—and one of these later won the Nobel Prize. Those I didn't care for were eventually sent to the country.

(or)

(Low Self-Evaluation) I thought most of my professors were geniuses—what they said always used to impress me.

To summarize, there were two separate experiments differing only in the direction of an interviewer's self-evaluation. In his relation to the student respondent, the interviewer was completely nonevaluative. In one experiment, his self-evaluation was excessively positive. In a second experiment, which was run concurrently, his self-evaluation was extremely modest and even negative. The prediction was that the subjects would negatively evaluate the interviewer when he overevaluated himself in relation to his professional status and positively evaluate the interviewer when he underevaluated himself.

THE INTERVIEWER'S PROFESSIONAL STANDING

The data provide evidence that the status manipulations had the intended effect. The specific measure was the rating of the interviewer's standing in his profession. In translation, the question read: "In your judgment, how important is the interviewer in his field?" There were six graded responses possible, ranging from "He is almost at the top of his field—surely in the upper 5 per cent" (scored 1) to "He is one of those who are least important in their field" (scored 6). The average estimates of the interviewer's importance are given in Table 11.

TABLE 11
MEAN IMPORTANCE RATING OF INTERVIEWER AS A FUNCTION OF
HIS SELF-EVALUATION AND STATUS

Interviewer's Self-Evaluation	*High Status*	*Low Status*	*Mann-Whitney U Test‡*
High	2.19*	3.05	$p < .01$
	$(N = 21)$†	$(N = 22)$	
Low	2.06	3.28	$p < .005$
	$(N = 16)$	$(N = 14)$	

* The lower the rating, the higher the estimated importance of the interviewer.

† Two subjects in the *Low-Status–High-Self-Evaluation* condition, two in the *High-Status–Low-Self-Evaluation* condition, and one in each of the remaining conditions did not make a status rating.

‡ Since the distributions were somewhat skewed, it was felt that a nonparametric test would be more justified than parametric t-tests.

It can be seen that the *High-Status* interviewer is regarded as more important in his field than the *Low-Status* interviewer under both conditions of self-evaluation. There is reason to believe, therefore, that the status manipulation was successful.

QUANTITATIVE EVALUATION

A first test of the hypothesis was based upon the attractiveness rating of the interviewer. There were six graded responses to the item which read: "How likable do you find the interviewer?" "I find him especially likable" was scored 1, whereas a score of 6 was given to "I find him especially unlikable."[3] The average attractiveness of the interviewer under the experimental conditions, as reflected by these ratings, is shown in Table 12.

TABLE 12
MEAN ATTRACTIVENESS RATING OF INTERVIEWER AS A FUNCTION OF HIS SELF-EVALUATION AND STATUS

| | Interviewer's Self-Evaluation | |
Interviewer's status	High	Low
High	2.77*	2.23†
	($N = 22$)	($N = 17$)
Low	3.08	3.13
	($N = 24$)	($N = 15$)
Mann-Whitney U Test	$p < .02$	$p < .02$

* The higher the rating, the more negative the evaluation of the interviewer.

† One subject did not make rating.

When the interviewer expresses a self-evaluation which is higher than the estimate of his worth provided by his low professional status, the evaluation of him is significantly lower than when his self-evaluation more closely corresponds to his status. On the other hand, when the interviewer expresses a self-evaluation which is markedly below the objective level inferred from his high-status position, the evaluation of him is significantly more positive than when his expressed self-evaluation is essentially in line with his professional status. Both sets of results are thus consistent with the experimental hypothesis.

It should be noted also that the *High-Status* interviewer who is self-depreciating tends to be evaluated more positively than

3. In Dutch, these six alternatives were defined by the terms *sympathiek* and *antipathiek*, which mean likable or nice and their opposites.

the *High-Status* interviewer who is rather boastful. Although this difference misses statistical significance, it appears to reflect the hypothesized tendency of subjects to reject the interviewer's invalid self-evaluation and to accept the more correct estimate based upon his high professional status. The weakness of the tendency could be due to the simultaneous presence of an opposing tendency to dislike self-depreciation. Perhaps the rather pointed display of inferiority feelings by the interviewer was somewhat distasteful to the subjects. This possibility is made more plausible by the fact that, in the *Low-Status* condition, the self-depreciating interviewer was disliked as much as the boastful one.

QUALITATIVE DATA

A second test of the validation hypothesis was based on the spontaneous reactions to the interviewer, which were given directly after the latter's departure. It will be recalled that, after being told about the impressions-of-personality study, subjects were asked simply to jot down their attitudes and feelings toward the interviewer.

After translating this material, a subsample of the combined experimental conditions was drawn at random from the total sample. Three readily identifiable categories were defined:

Neutral Evaluation

> Statements about the interviewer which fell into this category were nonevaluative or mildly positive descriptions of the interviewer's physical appearance, including dress and bearing and manner. For example:
> ... a quiet person.
> ... a practical psychologist.
> ... matter of fact.

Positive Evaluation

> Included in this category were explicitly positive evaluations of the interviewer. The statements refer to

his ability and intelligence, his moral stature, and other obviously attractive personality characteristics. For example:

... a hard worker in spite of what he knows already.
... a good person.
He is highly intelligent.

Negative Evaluation

The statements in this category are unequivocally negative. They covered many sides and dimensions of the interviewer's personality and behavior in the situation. For example:

He is not someone to have a nice party with.
... dull.
... he is impolite.
... a rather unpleasant person.

A total agreement of over 86 per cent was reached in the categorizing of the same data by a second, independent analyzer.

Table 13 contains the mean frequency of classified spontaneous evaluations under the experimental conditions.

TABLE 13
MEAN NUMBER OF QUALITATIVE EVALUATIONS
OF THE INTERVIEWER

	High Self-Evaluation				Low Self-Evaluation		
	High Status (N = 22)	*Low Status* (N = 24)			*High Status* (N = 18)	*Low Status* (N = 13)†	
Neutral	2.13	.79	p < .04*		1.27	.84	
Positive	1.68	1.88			2.61	1.84	
Negative	.91	1.54	p < .005		.66	1.53	p < .10

	High Status			Low Status	
	High SE‡	*Low SE*		*High SE*	*Low SE*
Neutral	2.13	1.27		.79	.84
Positive	1.68	2.61	p < .001	1.88	1.84
Negative	.91	.66		1.54	1.53

* All tests of significance are based on the Mann-Whitney U statistic.
† Two subjects did not respond.
‡ Self-evaluation.

In the situation where the interviewer is boastful but has low professional status, there are fewer neutral (or mildly positive) and many more negative evaluations of him than when he has high professional status. The evaluations of the *High-Status* interviewer who is self-depreciating tend to be more frequently neutral or positive and less frequently negative than those of the self-depreciating *Low-Status* interviewer. Although not as strong as desired in terms of statistical reliability, the differences between status conditions in the attractiveness of the interviewer are fully consistent with the pattern of evaluations reflected by the quantitative ratings (Table 12).

The differences within status conditions can easily be seen in the lower section of Table 13, where the data have been regrouped. The *High-Status* interviewer who is self-depreciating is considerably more attractive, in terms of frequency of positive evaluations, than the immodest interviewer of *High Status*. He is also less negative in terms of qualitative evaluations, although not significantly so. These results are in line with the validation hypothesis—subjects reject the modest self-evaluation and accept the more valid estimate given by the interviewer's high professional status. There is no evidence, however, of a validation tendency as far as the *Low-Status* interviewer is concerned. Here, subjects would be expected to evaluate the boastful interviewer more negatively than the self-depreciating one. A negative attitude toward self-depreciation itself does not seem to wholly account for the lack of a difference, since, as we have just seen, the self-depreciating, *High-Status* interviewer was *more* attractive than the boastful *High-Status* interviewer. But a negative attitude toward low status as such could account for the lack of a difference between the two types of *Low-Status* interviewers. Indeed, a negative attitude toward low status could also account for the more negative evaluation of the *Low-Status* boastful interviewer than of the *High-Status* one.

It is clearly necessary to rule out status as the exclusive determinant of these evaluations. The following logic seems to be sufficient. If the evaluation of the interviewer is found to vary with the degree to which the latter's expressed self-evaluation departs from a valid estimate of his objective valuation represented by a constant *Low-Status* position, a negative attitude toward low status as such cannot wholly explain the attractiveness of the interviewer. Furthermore, since there is some indication that a dislike of self-depreciation might have contributed *partially* to the lack of difference in attractiveness between the boastful and self-depreciating *Low-Status* interviewers, a more clinching case for the validation hypothesis can be made if the interviewer avoids self-depreciation altogether.

In line with these considerations, an experiment was designed in which the interviewer held a *Low-Status* position and expressed a *moderate* self-evaluation. It was expected that he would be evaluated more positively than the *Low-Status* interviewer in the original experiment, who was boastful. The experiment was conducted under identical physical and social conditions, employing the same general procedures and measures as in the original experiments. The subjects were drawn from the same pool of volunteer students. The questions asked of the confederate and the answers given by him were also exactly the same as in the basic experiments. However, the seven interpolated remarks, designed to express the interviewer's self-evaluation, were different. As can be seen, they are *moderately* positive as compared with the rather excessive evaluations expressed in the basic experiment. At the same time, the remarks in no way convey a self-depreciating attitude.

1. I speak a little French and German, but no Dutch.
2. I'm not a world traveler, but I've been to a couple of countries in the past six months.
3. I read a novel every now and then but would like to read more.
4. I once read *War and Peace* over a period of some weeks.
5. I've argued that both are important.
6. My capacity for work is about average; I can go pretty long without sleep.
7. Some [professors] I've had were good; others bad.

The interviewer (the same individual as in the two basic experiments) who expressed this moderate self-evaluation was introduced as having *Low Status,* using exactly the same verbal description as in the basic experiment. To summarize: If we can assume that a *Low-Status* interviewer who expresses a moderately high self-evaluation departs from "reality" *less* than a *Low-Status* interviewer who expresses a very high positive self-evaluation, the subject should be expected to evaluate him less negatively.

TABLE 14

MEAN ATTRACTIVENESS RATING AND QUALITATIVE EVALUATION
OF INTERVIEWER WITH LOW STATUS AND HIGH
OR MODERATE SELF-EVALUATION

Interviewer's Self- Evaluation	*Attractiveness* Rating	*Spontaneous Evaluation*		
		neutral	positive	negative
High	3.08*	.79	1.88	1.54
(N = 24)				
Moderate	2.33	1.33	2.00	1.00
(N = 15)				
Mann-Whitney U Test	p < .02			

* The smaller the number, the higher the attractiveness rating.

Table 14 shows this deduction to be correct insofar as the quantitative ratings are concerned. The evaluation of the moderate interviewer is significantly less negative than the evaluation of the interviewer who expresses a very high self-evaluation. The average frequency of classified evaluations presented on the right side of Table 14 is consistent with the quantitative ratings. Although the differences do not attain statistical significance, the directional pattern always conforms to the expected pattern. Over-all, the conclusion seems fairly justified that the negative evaluation of the interviewer is a function of the discrepancy between his expressed self-evaluation and his professional status and not due to the subject's attitude toward status alone. Thus, the explanation of attractiveness in terms of a need to maintain social valuations in accord with an objective estimate accounts parsimoniously for differences in evaluations of a person whose professional status varies but whose expressed self-evaluation is constant, as well as for the differences in the evaluation of a person whose status is constant but whose expressed self-evaluation varies.

7 The Reaction to Positive and Negative Biases

There has been a plaguing problem in the interpretation of the experimental data thus far considered. Although an attitude toward status—for example, admiration of people who enjoy high prestige—could not alone have accounted for the attractiveness of the interviewer, this factor could have been contributory. Similarly, although neither a dislike of conceit nor a distaste for publicly exposed inferiority feelings could have exclusively determined the attractiveness of the interviewer, there is a possibility that these attitudes were partly responsible. If such were the case, the conclusion that the hypothesized validation motive did not entirely determine the subject's evaluation of the interviewer would not be bothersome at all. Obviously, there are many determinants of attraction and hostility. The problem,

123

however, is to prove unequivocally that a cognitive-validation process is *one* of the multiple determinants. Concerning this objective, we must frankly admit that our arguments still contain weaknesses which have to be considered and dealt with. As mentioned earlier, a status-linked attitude might have been operating to determine attractiveness when the interviewer's expressed self-evaluation was held constant, and a negative attitude toward the interviewer's conceit as such might have been operating to determine his attractiveness when his professional status was held constant. Thus, one could argue that the positive and negative evaluations of the interviewer were the result of two *independent* determinants. When one of these was held constant, the other was free to affect the interviewer's attractiveness. In order to confirm the validation hypothesis, it is necessary to show that the subject is reacting to the *discrepancy* between the valid and invalid estimates of the interviewer's valuation which are available to him in the interaction situation. Some such direct evidence was presented in Chapter 5. There, it was shown that the evaluation of the interviewer varied with the perceived legitimacy of his expressed high self-evaluation. That is, the greater the discrepancy perceived by the subject between the interviewer's self-evaluation and his "true" worth, the more negative the evaluation of him. But this was essentially internal, correlational evidence and, consequently, not entirely conclusive. We would surely be on firmer ground if neither the attitude toward status alone nor the attitude toward boastfulness alone could be invoked even as a partial determinant of another person's attractiveness. An altogether different methodological tack, along the following lines, may help reduce the area of ambiguity surrounding our research results.

The basic elements of the validation process which theoretically operates in interpersonal attraction and hostility are estimates of another person's valuation along some dimension. We have employed the person's self-evaluation as the invalid estimate and his professional status as the valid estimate of his valuation. These estimates, however, are not the only ones that could have been used to generate a validation process. The person himself did not have to be a source of information about his own worth. An estimate of the person's worth can be given by a third party who is relevant to the relationship between the subject and the person whom he evaluates. If this source is judged to be biased, the hypothesized validation motivation should be aroused. Accordingly, the attractiveness of the person evaluated should reflect a rejection of the presumably invalid estimate given by the biased party. In this formulation of the experimental question, it should be noted that the person's conceit is not involved at all in the subject's evaluation of him. Equally, the person's status cannot be a factor. Rather, the attractiveness of the person would seem to be determined only by the validity of the estimate, provided by someone else, of his valuation. Based upon such a theoretical analysis, the first of several experiments was expected to show that, if a negatively biased informant evaluates a person negatively, the person will tend to be less unattractive than if he is evaluated negatively by an unbiased informant.

PROCEDURE AND MEASURES

Volunteer females from various undergraduate classes served as subjects. Three or four girls were seated in separate booths and received the following instructions:

> The study in which you will participate today is concerned with the formation of first impressions. We all know that, in real life, we often have to make evaluations of other people when there is only a small amount of information to go on. More than that, we have deep emotional reactions to others without having had much, if any, face-to-face contact with them. It is not only true for the romantic heroes of literature that intense love or hatred can be generated toward a person without any experience with that person. There is no question that likes and dislikes are based on an intuitive picture of a person, developed from fragments of information.
>
> Today, we would like to obtain your reactions to

a fellow student on the basis of information provided by another person in an interview. We want to know how much you like or dislike him.

Each of you has two buttons in front of you, mounted on a small wooden stand. As you listen to the informant give her views about the student— named Harry, by the way—on this tape which I'm going to play, you will be developing a picture of him. During this picture development, you will experience positive or negative feelings about the student. These feelings may be weak or highly intense; they may be fleeting or sustained and cumulative. What we'd like you to do is to register these feelings by pressing the appropriate button an appropriate number of times. At the very instant that you have a negative feeling, press the negative button, no matter how weak or transient that feeling. Similarly, the moment you have a positive feeling or image, press the positive button. Press the buttons as often as is necessary to register all of your reactions as they are developing. A strong reaction or impression is worth several weak ones, so the stronger each single reaction is, the more times you should press the button, since each press counts only one unit. Please don't be inhibited; we are not concerned with you as an identifiable individual. In fact, your scores will be known to us only by number.

Now in the case of the student to whom you're going to react, we've been able to get only one informant who will provide information about him. We can't tell you much about the informant except to say that. . . .

At this point, the validity of the estimate of the student's valuation was manipulated by giving the subject information about the informant, from which she could infer that the estimate was either negatively biased or unbiased. Specifically, the negative bias was introduced by way of the following remarks:

We can't tell you much about the informant except to say that her name is Claire, and she is Harry's former fiancée. They were engaged, but they broke off the engagement a couple of weeks back, amicably, we understood. However, when we talked with her, Claire seemed to have become quite emotional on the subject of Harry and the engagement. She had evidently undergone some kind of a change. Despite this, Claire said she was certainly qualified to supply information on Harry.

The *Unbiased* condition was created by describing the following informant:

We can't tell you much about the informant except to say her name is Claire, and she happens to be the wife of a camp director with whom Harry worked last summer. Harry and Claire worked together at camp, and Claire got to know Harry pretty well—they still have frequent contact. Claire happens to be a very good clinical psychologist who was recommended to us as a good, objective observer for this experiment.

After one of the above sets of remarks about the informant, the subject's attention was called to a card with a set of evaluation categories. In order to avoid suspicion about the rather detailed and negative evaluation that they were about to hear, subjects were told that Claire had used an identical outline in preparing and delivering her oral report on Harry. Following a final request to press the positive or negative button whenever an evaluative impulse occurred, Claire's taped remarks about Harry were presented. The button presses activated simple electric counters in an adjacent room. The information about Harry which the subjects heard was exactly as follows:

You want a physical description first—Harry's about average height—certainly no more than just average. He's on the skinny side, too. He has light brown hair, a little sparse already, and, I would say, sort of muddy blue eyes. Let's see—posture. Well, Harry slouches, and he has very round shoulders. Oh yes, his walk is funny. It looks as if he's chasing something.

As for ability, I don't think Harry's terribly bright. He never seemed to have much information about current events—you know, politics and international relations. He did talk a lot about the Cuban crisis—got very involved in it, but I thought his views were superficial. He reads a lot, especially biography, but he doesn't go deeply into a book. He knows the characters and the plots, but not what's underneath—what makes the people move. I don't know—he misses—oh well. . . .

What's his personality like? I think he's a completely self-centered person—he rarely asks for someone else's opinion or whether he could be helpful and do something for you. He appears friendly with that grin, but he's really out for himself. Harry lacks social poise—he feels uncomfortable with others and makes them feel uncomfortable. Fundamentally, I don't think he likes people. Oh, he has friends, but fewer than the average fellow. Besides, I don't think he's really close to anyone.

Sincerity? Well, I just think he's a dishonest person. He never lets you know how he feels, or he tells you the opposite of what he feels. He would say: I enjoyed this very much, then the next time you'd see him, he'd complain.

As to his personal appearance, he's not a neat dresser. In fact, he was pretty sloppy at times. Oh yes, on the personality question, Harry is not very generous. He would always count his pennies. And he really didn't need to. He was earning some money, and, besides, he doesn't come from a poor family. They would contribute now and then.

His interests? Well, his taste in things like art and music is pretty bad. He goes to concerts and art exhibits, but he doesn't know much about the things he sees or hears. He says he likes art, but his tastes aren't very refined.

Groups and leadership? Well, Harry is not a leader. He belongs to some school groups and clubs, but he belongs in order to gain prestige. Harry's just the type to do that.

As you can gather, my over-all impression of Harry is pretty negative. I don't think he's a decent human being.

The same tape, of course, was used for both the *Negatively Biased* and *Unbiased* conditions. It lasted approximately five minutes. In order to prevent subjects from hearing each other's buttons being pressed, metronomes, clocks, and a fan were operated. At the conclusion of the tape, the button-pressing data being in, subjects were asked to jot down their over-all impressions of Harry. Then, after three minutes, an over-all impression of Claire was requested. The experiment was finished three minutes later. A full explanation of the purposes and stratagems was given before subjects were finally dismissed.

IDENTIFICATION OF NEGATIVE BIAS

Data on the subject's impression of Claire were collected in order to determine whether she was seen as a biased or an unbiased informant in line with the experimental manipulation. The impressions were examined, and a simple tabulation was made of the number of subjects in each experimental condition who explicitly stated or strongly implied that Claire was a biased informant. An independent tabulation agreed 85 per cent with the original one. It is evident from Table 15 that, when the informant is described as Harry's ex-fiancée, there are considerably more subjects who regard her as biased than when she is described as a clinical psychologist. If it can be assumed that the validity of a negative estimate of the student's worth corresponds to the objectivity of the source of the estimate, then the intended experimental conditions were, in fact, created.

TABLE 15

NUMBER OF SUBJECTS WHO IDENTIFY INFORMANT'S
NEGATIVE BIAS

Experimental Condition	Bias Mentioned	Bias Not Mentioned
Negatively Biased ($N = 24$)	21	3
Unbiased ($N = 24$)	10	14

$$\chi^2 \ (1 \ df) = 11.00$$
$$p < .001$$

QUANTITATIVE EVALUATIONS OF A REPORTEDLY UNATTRACTIVE PERSON

How much the subject liked Harry can be inferred from the number of times she pressed the negative and positive buttons as she listened to the tape. The mean numbers of button presses under the *Negatively Biased* and *Unbiased* conditions are given in Table 16.

TABLE 16

MEAN NUMBER OF NEGATIVE AND POSITIVE BUTTON PRESSES,
GIVEN BIASED OR UNBIASED INFORMANT WHO MAKES
NEGATIVE EVALUATION OF HARRY

Experimental Conditions	Buttons Pressed	
	Negative	Positive
Negatively Biased ($N = 24$)	16.9	3.2
Unbiased ($N = 24$)	25.9	3.0

$$t = 2.00$$
$$p < .05$$

Although exactly the same evaluative information about Harry was provided, the subject finds him quite a bit more unattractive when the information comes from an unbiased informant. This finding would seem to support the view that the estimate of Harry's valuation tended to be rejected as invalid or accepted as valid according to the objectivity of the source of the estimate. Insofar as button-pressing is a measure of attraction, then, the data tend to confirm the validation hypothesis.

QUALITATIVE EVALUATIONS OF A REPORTEDLY UNATTRACTIVE PERSON

An examination of the qualitative impressions of Harry, which the subject recorded after the tape had been played, showed unmistakably that there had been strong personal reactions to Harry. Some individuals began by denouncing Harry and ended up being more moderate and even sympathetic in their evaluations. Others made no qualifications; they were unequivocally negative. Since, in either case, it was difficult to score the degree to which any subject felt negative, the number of subjects who were unqualifiedly negative about Harry was tabulated and compared with the number who were positive or slightly and qualifiedly negative under each experimental condition. Reliability in terms of an independent coding of this material approached 81 per cent. Table 17 shows the number of subjects who fall into each of these exhaustive categories.

TABLE 17

NUMBER OF SUBJECTS WHO MAKE NEGATIVE OR QUALIFIEDLY NEGATIVE EVALUATIONS OF HARRY UNDER BIASED AND UNBIASED CONDITIONS

Experimental Conditions	Qualitative Impressions of Harry	
	Negative	*Qualifiedly Negative or Positive*
Unbiased (N = 24)	16	8
Negatively Biased (N = 24)	3	21

$$\chi^2 \text{ (1 df)} = 14.60$$
$$p < .001$$

There are fewer subjects who express purely negative attitudes toward Harry when he is described by a negatively biased informant. Under the latter condition, more than 80 per cent of the subjects make positive evaluations or negative ones which are highly qualified. These findings are entirely consistent with the button-pressing data and reinforce the interpretation of those data.

SYMMETRY IN COGNITIVE VALIDATION

If an underlying validation process shows itself in the rejection of an estimated valuation provided by a negatively biased informant, it should also be reflected under conditions of positive bias. When an informant who makes a highly positive evaluation of a person is regarded as prejudiced in the person's favor, the subject should reject the estimate of valuation provided by this source. Thus, the attractiveness of a person when he is evaluated by a positively biased source should be less than when he is evaluated by an unbiased source. An experiment to check this prediction followed exactly the same format used in the negative-bias study. A presumably positive bias in the informant was created by the following remarks, given to the subjects just prior to their listening to the informant's taped evaluation of Harry:

> We can't tell you much about the informant except to say that her name is Claire and she is Harry's fiancée. Claire and Harry met just a couple of months back and began immediately to date rather heavily. After sort of a whirlwind romance, they've become engaged and plan to marry as soon as possible. Claire was more than cooperative at the suggestion of giving her appraisal of Harry.

The unbiased informant was described in exactly the same terms as in the previous experiment: a camp director's wife and clinical psychologist who had worked with Harry during the summer. The positive evaluation recorded on tape by both the *Positively Biased* and *Unbiased* informants was as follows:

> You want a physical description first? Well, Harry's above-average height, has light brown hair, cut short,

and blue eyes. I certainly feel he's pleasant looking. He has a fresh, open expression, with a quick smile. As for posture, he's surely well-built and stands very straight. He's very athletic, you know, especially in basketball. Yes, Harry's certainly physically fit, and I guess you might call his sort of friendly, easy manner part of his description, also.

As for ability, Harry's a fairly good student. He has a keen and flexible mind. He likes to puzzle things out for himself. He always seems to have a lot of information about current events—you know, politics and international relations and things. I remember he talked a lot about the Cuban crisis and really got very involved in it. That's another thing—people respect his opinions about things.

He reads a lot, especially biography. Harry can read a book through at an amazing rate and then summarize it right to the point and even tell you what the author was writing between the lines, so to speak. He's very perceptive that way.

What's his personality like? Well, Harry's fundamentally a warm and engaging person. Something about his friendly smile tells you this and draws you to him. He certainly has social poise. He has that coveted ability to make other people feel comfortable with him. I know he has several good friends without being—well, excessively social, shall we say. If I were to rate his personality on a scale, he would be very positive in most categories.

Sincerity? Well—Harry has always proven to be honest with me. He's quite trustworthy; you can depend upon his word. He's discreet—the kind of person that you can trust with your personal problems. He'll always tell you just what he thinks about something, and I think that's important.

As to his personal appearance, I happen to know that Harry takes pride in being well-groomed. He may not be the best-dressed man on campus, but he is always neat. I would rate him high on this. Oh yes, by the way, on the personality question, I should mention Harry's generosity. With what time and money he has, I've always observed that he's willing to lend someone a hand. This is important, for it manifests deeper positive character traits.

Now, his interests? Well, I do admire his taste in things like art and music. I know he likes good art a lot and knows a lot about it. He has a good appreciation for most forms of art and music, without being hyperintellectual.

Groups and leadership—oh, I don't know. . . . I would say Harry really does his best to contribute to a group. As for leadership, it's hard to say. Harry displays the marks of a good leader. He's responsible, as you know by his activities in clubs and things, plus the work he did last summer.

Well, anyway, I guess you can gather that my overall impression of Harry is rather favorable. I don't really have anything that I want to record against him. Is that all?

IDENTIFICATION OF POSITIVE BIAS

The over-all impressions of Claire were examined for evidence that she was seen as positively biased. A simple tabulation was made of the number of subjects who explicitly mentioned or strongly implied that Claire was prejudiced in Harry's favor. Table 18 shows more mentions of bias under the *Positively Biased* than under the *Unbiased* condition. The experimental manipulations were, therefore, successful as far as the bias of the informant is concerned. If the validity of the positive estimate of Harry's worth can be assumed to be a function of the bias of Claire—the source of the estimate—then the experimental condition necessary to test the validation hypothesis can also be assumed to have been successfully induced.

TABLE 18

NUMBER OF SUBJECTS WHO IDENTIFY INFORMANT'S
POSITIVE BIAS

Experimental Condition	Bias Mentioned	Bias Not Mentioned
Positively Biased (N = 24)	11	13
Unbiased (N = 24)	3	21

$$\chi^2 \text{ (1 df)} = 6.40$$
$$p < .02$$

QUANTITATIVE EVALUATIONS OF A REPORTEDLY ATTRACTIVE PERSON

The evaluation of Harry, as measured by the number of times the positive and negative buttons were pressed while subjects listened to the tape recording of Claire's rather favorable description, is presented in Table 19. The evaluation is clearly less positive when the informant is positively biased than when she is unbiased. In theoretical terms, we may say that the estimate of Harry's valuation given by a positively biased source is rejected as invalid. Harry's relatively lower attractiveness under the *Positively Biased* condition presumably reflects this underlying validation process.

TABLE 19

MEAN NUMBER OF NEGATIVE AND POSITIVE BUTTON PRESSES BY
BIASED OR UNBIASED INFORMANTS WHO MAKE POSITIVE
EVALUATIONS OF HARRY

Experimental Conditions	Buttons Pressed	
	Negative	Positive
Positively Biased (N = 24)	2.5	25.54
Unbiased (N = 24)	2.0	37.88

$$t = 2.47$$
$$p < .01$$

QUALITATIVE EVALUATIONS OF A REPORTEDLY ATTRACTIVE PERSON

Just as in the case of the negative-bias study, the over-all impressions of Harry, written after the button-pressing period, reveal strong positive feelings about him. Some subjects, however, qualified their positive evaluations somewhat or were actually critical in various ways. Subjects under each experimental condition were easily classified as making an unequivocally positive evaluation or a qualified positive evaluation. An independent tabulation in terms of these exhaustive categories agreed 84 per cent with the original tabulation. Table 20 makes evident that Harry is less attractive when the source of information about him—on which the evaluation is presumably based—is positively biased. Thus, the qualitative impressions are fully consistent with the button-pressing data.

TABLE 20

NUMBER OF SUBJECTS WHO MAKE POSITIVE OR QUALIFIEDLY POSITIVE EVALUATIONS OF HARRY UNDER BIASED AND UNBIASED CONDITIONS

	Qualitative Impressions of Harry	
Experimental Conditions	Positive	Qualifiedly Positive or Negative
Unbiased (N = 24)	18	6
Positively Biased (N = 24)	9	15

$$\chi^2 \text{ (1 df)} = 6.86$$
$$p < .01$$

ASSESSMENT

In assessing the evidence in support of the validation hypothesis, it is important to bear in mind that both measures of attractiveness—the button-pressing and the qualitative impressions—were spontaneous and uninfluenced by any external pressures. That is, the experimenter in no way suggested that the bias be taken into account in the formation of evaluative impressions. Nor was there any reward explicit or implied for the making of accurate evaluations. Thus, there is reason to suppose that attractiveness was directly affected by the validity of the valuation estimate contained in the informant's taped remarks.

There is, however, one point about the interpretation that needs to be considered, at least in the negative-bias study. It could be argued that, when the subject is given information on which she bases her evaluation, she reacts to the informant. For example, the bias of the informant might have been a disliked characteristic, and the subject might have looked favorably on Harry out of contrast with the unattractive informant. Or, apart from her attitude toward the bias itself, the subject might have felt sorry for Harry for having had to put up with such a perfectionistic and domineering creature as Claire. It would seem that, for these explanations to be compelling, the negatively biased informant would have had to be seen as more unattractive than the unbiased informant. Examination of the qualitative impressions which subjects had of Claire does show that she is slightly (but not significantly) more unattractive when she is biased than when she is unbiased. However, if it is argued that subjects think less negatively of Harry on the basis of his contrast with the disliked Claire, such an interpretation cannot be applied equally to the positive-bias experiment. In this case, Claire was disliked more when she was biased than when she was unbiased. Yet, Harry is *less* attractive under the *Positively Biased* condition than under the *Unbiased* condition. On the other hand, it cannot be argued consistently that Harry's attraction is directly influenced by Claire's attraction. If this was the case when Claire was positively biased, it was not the case when Claire was negatively biased. There is, then, no compelling evidence that the attractiveness of Harry was determined by the attractiveness of Claire.

CHANGE TOWARD A VALID EVALUATION

In essence, the strategy pursued thus far has been to compare the attractiveness of a person across experimental conditions in

which estimates of the person's worth have been systematically
varied as to their validity. For example, the attractiveness of a
person whose self-evaluation exceeded his professional status
was compared with his attractiveness when his self-evaluation
matched his status. Similarly, the evaluation of a person described by a biased informant was compared with the evaluation
of him when he was described by an unbiased informant. Such
comparisons between experimental conditions have permitted
the inference of the existence of an underlying cognitive-validation process. The inference, however, is an indirect one, based
upon two sets of subjects who perceive different amounts of
validity in estimates of a particular person's valuation. A more
direct reflection of a validation process would consist in showing that individuals *change* their evaluations of other persons
in response to information pertaining to the validity of their
existing valuations. If a person's attraction can be shown to
rise or fall depending upon the validity of the estimates of that
person's worth, a much more direct confirmation of the hypothesis will have been achieved. Accordingly, an experiment
was designed so that subjects listened to an evaluation of a
certain person by a third party and formed their own evaluative
impressions of the person. Then, they were given information
relevant to the validity of the valuations. Then, finally, they
evaluated the person while hearing the informant's evaluation
a second time. If attraction is a reflection of the tendency to
maintain a valid cognitive structure, changes in the latter toward
greater validity should be reflected in increased or lowered attractiveness.

In the first "change" experiment, subjects listened to the
same five-minute negative evaluation of Harry that had been
employed in the original experiment. Then the experimenter
suddenly recalled that he had forgotten to mention who the
informant was and that he was obliged to do this. The idea was
to create the impression that there was some from of quasi-legal
requirement to reveal the source of information about persons
in these interviews. He perfunctorily told the subjects:

Her name is Claire. She was engaged to be married to Harry's cousin, and that is why she knows Harry. When we spoke to Claire she was very wrought up and emotional because she had just learned that her fiancé —Harry's cousin—had eloped with another girl. A couple of days later, while denouncing the male component of the human race, she agreed to tape her observations about Harry—which you will now hear again.

Two essential features of this characterization of Claire should be noted. First, Claire had not been involved in a relationship with Harry. Hence, subjects could not feel sorry for his having had to put up with her. Second, the circumstances leading to the development of a negative bias toward *all* men were apparently beyond Claire's control. Her being suddenly jilted was a cruel blow for which she could not be held primarily responsible. Rather than dislike her intensely, as some subjects did in the original study, subjects should be expected to feel more tolerant toward her. This attitude should also counteract the distaste for Claire's prejudice and, thus, should reduce any tendency to evaluate Harry sympathetically out of contrast.

As for the negative bias of Claire, it was explicitly mentioned or strongly implied by 85 per cent of the subjects in their informal impressions of her written after the second hearing of the tape. As before, we may take this to mean that the estimate of Harry's worth which the subject had already made was now considered to be invalid.

CHANGES IN ATTRACTIVENESS

The number of net negative (number negative minus number positive) button presses made before and after receipt of the information concerning Claire's negative prejudice is given in Table 21.

It is evident that, after learning of Claire's identity and particularly of her negative bias, the average subject found

TABLE 21

MEAN NUMBER OF NET NEGATIVE BUTTON PRESSES BEFORE AND
AFTER KNOWLEDGE OF INFORMANT'S NEGATIVE BIAS

	Informant's Negative Evaluation of Harry	
	First Hearing	*Second Hearing*
Subject's Evaluation of Harry (N = 20)	− 16.0	− .4

t diff. = 2.26
p < .05

Harry considerably less unattractive. This finding is consistent
with the view that, when the validity of an existing estimate of
valuation changes, the attractiveness of that person will change
in a direction reflecting greater validity.

If a negative bias of the informant causes the subject to
make a less negative evaluation of Harry, a positive bias should
cause Harry to become less attractive. An experiment was run
to check this prediction, employing the same before-after design
as used in the negative-bias–change study. The information
given to the subject about Claire to create the impression that
she was positively biased was the same as that employed in the
original experiment in which a biased condition was compared
with an unbiased condition. The number of net positive button
presses before and after the knowledge of the positive bias is
given in Table 22.

TABLE 22

MEAN NUMBER OF NET POSITIVE BUTTON PRESSES BEFORE AND
AFTER KNOWLEDGE OF INFORMANT'S POSITIVE BIAS

	Informant's Positive Evaluation of Harry	
	First Hearing	*Second Hearing*
Subject's Evaluation of Harry (N = 20)	+ 37.5	+ 19.5

t diff. = 1.83
p < .10

Although the statistical reliability of the change is not as high as we should like it, the trend strongly suggests that Harry has sustained a loss of attractiveness. The fact that, here, there is a *loss* of attractiveness, whereas, in the case of the negative-bias study, there was a net *gain* in attractiveness, shows that the mere repetition of the tape could not have been responsible for the changes.

8 Cognitive Validation and Self-Evaluation

The experimental program described thus far has been concerned wholly with the individual's evaluations of other persons. We are now prepared to shift our focus to self-evaluation. In this perspective, the theoretical question arises: Can the validation hypothesis which has been applied to the evaluation of other persons also be applied to the evaluation of the self? If the individual's existing estimate of himself in a given domain is lower or higher than it ought to be according to a dependable objective criterion, does he alter that estimate so that it becomes more valid?

From the viewpoint of private experience, it is clear that what one considers to be one's worth in most intellectual and moral spheres depends upon how one's conduct compares with relevant objective and social standards. Thus, for example, success or failure in achieving goals of recognized social value causes the individual's estimate of his valid worth to move correspondingly upward or downward. Similarly, if his conduct falls above or below the level prescribed by social norms, he will estimate his apparent objective worth to be correspondingly higher or lower than his existing self-evaluation. If the concept of cognitive validation can be applied to the self, a general hypothesis can be formulated as follows: If the individual's conduct brings about a discrepancy between his existing self-evaluation and his estimate of his objective worth—that is, how good or bad he thinks he really is—there is a tendency for him to raise or lower his self-evaluation so that it conforms more closely to the objective estimate.

Research which aims to test this general hypothesis, as it is defined in a concrete experimental setting, requires a different methodology from that used to test social-evaluation hypotheses. When dealing with the evaluation of others, the paramount methodological problem was to hold constant or to eliminate social motives like status and security. In essence, such controls were established by preventing other persons from threatening or rewarding the subject with respect to his status and security. But when focusing on self-evaluation, the control of interfering motives becomes more difficult. Often, when the individual's evaluation of himself differs from a reliable estimate of his objective worth—and thus needs to be validated or "corrected"—he also becomes simultaneously motivated to protect his self-esteem. For example, if an individual violates certain moral or ethical norms of conduct, his existing self-evaluation is regarded as, at least temporarily, higher than it should be. In response to the need for cognitive validation, he tends to lower his self-evaluation. But the tendency to devalue himself generates an opposing tendency to preserve his self-esteem. Under these circumstances, there would seem to be only one way of testing validation hypotheses about the self: *to focus upon the direction in which a self-evaluation conflict is resolved.*

Given this general strategy, the next theoretical question

is: What governs the direction in which a self-evaluation conflict is resolved? A general and intuitively plausible answer is
that whether the individual actually lowers his self-evaluation
to a more valid level or maintains his self-esteem depends upon
his being able to deny the norm-violating conduct or his responsibility for it. If the situation allows him this denial, the need
for a corrective self-devaluation is obviated, and his self-esteem
is maintained.

A preliminary experiment was conducted in order to gather
information on an induced self-evaluation conflict which would
lead to a later test of a quantitative hypothesis. The experimental
design aimed at creating the perception in the subject that he
had excessively and undeniably hurt another person. It was
assumed that such conduct would constitute a deviation from,
or violation of, various internal norms which were pertinent to
the subject's self-evaluation. And, since his norm-violating conduct was likely to be undeniable, it was expected that the subject would show some evidence of lowered self-attractiveness,
partly reflecting the downward correction of his existing self-
evaluation to a more valid level.

PROCEDURE AND MEASURES

Students from various undergraduate courses were invited
to participate in a mental-health research program. They were
told that the objective of the program was to evaluate a new
approach to psychotherapy: They would help diagnose the
personal problems of a student who had sought help from the
university clinic. The underlying rationale for this new therapeutic approach was that peers could often better identify with
a troubled student than a professional therapist could. They
could intuit the essence of the problem more quickly and, at
the same time, permit the troubled student to talk freely about
the things that bothered him most deeply.

Following these orienting remarks, the subject and two
other students, who were actually confederates, were handed a
case history of another student who had come to the university

clinic for help. To ensure that the subject grasped the details of the case, the experimenter read aloud the following excerpted statement:

CARTER FENWICK
No. 40727

Carter P. Fenwick comes from an upper-middle-class American family. . . . He had an indulgent upbringing. In the fourth grade, he created an unpleasant disturbance by refusing to sit in the same classroom with a Negro girl.

Carter was dissatisfied about going to Penn; he originally wanted to go to Brown or Princeton. During his first year, he maintained an attitude of aloofness toward his fellow students. . . . Those students with whom he did form close associations were those who could be of special help to him or instrumental to him in times of difficulty—such as during final examinations—or those who could gain entrance for him to the proper social circles. At one point, Carter attempted to force dormitory officials to remove his roommate. This was to no avail, so he resorted to spreading fictions and defamatory stories about him.

For his second year, his father saw to it that Carter was accepted as a pledge in his old fraternity. Not long after his arrival, a sizable sum of money was stolen from the fraternity strongbox. Carter pointed out that his roommate had recently acquired a considerable sum of money. A large portion of the missing money was found in the roommate's locker. Carter testified that his roommate was definitely responsible for the theft. . . . The fraternity suspended the roommate, and he was expelled from the university.

Carter became involved with a group which planned racial episodes in Philadelphia. A noted hatemonger was at the head of this group, which directed its efforts against Negroes, Jews, and Catholics.

Carter came to know his new roommate's girl friend, with whom he had an intimate relationship for several months. When she informed him that she had become pregnant, he immediately dissociated himself from her and, despite her pleadings, refused to see her. The girl, in desperation, had an abortion performed, resulting in irreparable physical damage to her. When word of this got back to Carter's mother, she became extremely distraught and suffered a nervous breakdown. She is now in a private sanatorium.

Carter took up with other girls immediately after this incident. It was under the influence of his current girl friend that he came for aid, although he insisted that his actions were constantly being misjudged and that people did not appreciate his very high abilities. However, she insisted that they could not continue their relationship if he did not change his behavior.

The object of the case history was to get the subject to develop and openly express strong and righteous criticism of Carter, the problem student. To assure this, the subject presented his views within the framework of the following questions posed by the experimenter:

1. How would you characterize this individual?
2. Do you like him as a person?
3. What kind of relationship would you be able to develop with him?
4. Judging from his actions, what do you think are his goals in life?
5. What do you think of his character?
6. What do you suggest as to his suitability for marriage? . . . his ability to hold a responsible job? . . . his becoming a camp counselor? . . . his representing students on the student council?
7. How would you evaluate his attitude toward his family and friends?

The typical subject expressed strong condemnation in response to one or more of these questions. Moreover, by skillful probing during the questioning itself or by his summary of the subject's attitude at the end of the questioning, the interviewer brought out strong denunciations. Informal observations show that every subject, at some point, strongly denounced Carter's moral character.

The second subject, actually a confederate, was then interviewed, employing the same questions. However, these remarks were carefully prepared in advance to express tolerant and even sympathetic attitudes toward Carter. Two basic themes were used in this contrasting interview: 1) Carter is in trouble and knows it. He is actively seeking help and needs to be supported. 2) Carter has had difficulty in expressing himself, partly because he has been misunderstood. He certainly has not been helped by those who should have helped him and indeed seems to have been led astray by them. The confederate noted Carter's misdeeds but urged understanding, especially since, even if one person should judge another, not all of the facts of the case were known.

The point of this procedure was to bring the subject to think that his denunciation of Carter had been excessive. At the very least, the second student's remarks would show the subject that it is possible to interpret Carter in a different and perhaps more enlightened and mature way. To reinforce in the subject's mind the idea that he had undeniably violated a code of fair play and various other social and internal norms, the experimenter then introduced the third subject seated at the table as Carter Fenwick. The subject and the first confederate were told that Carter was present in order to learn how other people reacted to him. They were told that *most subjects* had definitely been supportive and encouraging and *this* would presumably be of therapeutic benefit.

Thus, all subjects were in the position of having made some form of denunciation of Carter and of knowing that the latter had heard it. For many subjects, criticizing someone whom they had not met was indecorous, undignified, and a breach of social etiquette. Others thought their conduct was reprehensible because they had condemned a fellow student who was emotionally unable to rise to his own defense and who, at this crucial juncture in his life, desperately needed a friend. Some subjects probably felt humiliated and embarrassed because they had been observed violating their ideals of fairness. Some subjects probably felt angry over being tricked, despite the plausible rationale for Carter's being there incognito. Finally, one may assume there were subjects who were afraid that Carter would in some way retaliate. To focus these conglomerate feelings and to reinforce the subject's belief that he had been excessively negative and harmful, Carter made a number of "spontaneous" remarks directly after his presence was revealed. Two opposing statements made to two randomly composed groups of subjects constituted the experimental conditions. In what can be called the *Hurt* condition, Carter strongly implied the kinds of norm deviations mentioned above: that the subject was thoughtless, inconsiderate, rash, discouraging, and even cruel in his comments, especially in ignoring the possibility that he was dealing with someone not altogether well emotionally. In a contrasting *Help* condition, Carter attempted to relieve the subject of any such feelings, implying that he now saw things in a more realistic light. In the *Hurt* condition, Carter was extremely distraught and on the verge of tears. The remarks in the two conditions were as follows:

Hurt Condition

> Nobody has ever said such bad things about me. . . . People like you, who don't give careful thought to what they say, make me feel very depressed. I felt terribly let down by your comments; I feel worse now than when I came in; this therapy session hasn't helped me at all; in fact, it makes me want to give this whole thing up and drop out; on the whole, these group-therapy sessions are good—I've really benefited from those in the past, but today I think I've really been set back. Somehow I feel back where I started.

Maybe it's because this group couldn't agree that I had possibilities.

Help Condition

I don't feel at all bad because of your comments. People have told me things like that before, and, in fact, I'm beginning to appreciate comments such as yours for their thoughtfulness. Your remarks gave me a big lift—a sort of before-after picture. In general, I'd like to say that I've derived much from these therapy sessions, which have helped me a great deal.

After his statement, Carter left the room. In the *Hurt* condition, the experimenter expressed disbelief and surprise at the turn of events. He then recovered and said that the procedure in the analysis of the case history, originally scheduled to occur later, would now take place. Subjects were requested to fill out a brief questionnaire. Absolute assurance was given that the information provided would not be seen by Carter or even by the experimenter until weeks later, when the data would be assembled, and that, in any case, the responses would be anonymous.

The questionnaire contained seven items: Four dealt with the subject's interpretation of his own conduct in discussing the case history, and three dealt with his evaluation of Carter. The response to each question was measured by a 21-unit rating scale. Following the questionnaire, the subjects evaluated themselves in terms of their favorable and unfavorable personality charactics. Finally, the subjects wrote memos incorporating their over-all views on the case.

At the conclusion of the experiment, each subject was given a thorough explanation of the purposes of the study, the procedures used, and the measures. The confederate who played the role of Carter introduced himself and spent some time explaining the problems he had in identifying with Carter. Care was taken that the subject understood the rationale for the deception and that he understood his own reactions to it.

To anticipate the interpretation of the data, it should be carefully noted that there was nothing in Carter's remarks to suggest that the subject was wrong in the substantive points he made in his diagnosis and criticism. The subject's grasp and interpretation of the facts described in the case history were not touched upon at all by Carter. Second, there was nothing in Carter's remarks which directed the subject to lower his estimate of his own attractiveness. The essence of Carter's statements was that the subject had or had not seriously hurt him.

QUESTIONNAIRE REACTIONS

Table 23 shows the mean ratings on the seven items of the questionnaire by subjects in the *Hurt* and *Help* conditions.

TABLE 23

MEAN QUESTIONNAIRE RATINGS UNDER HURT AND
HELP CONDITIONS

Items	*Hurt* (N = 19)	*Help* (N = 18)	
Effect on Carter's Morale	3.84	9.33	$t = 4.81, p < .002$
Ability as a Psychologist	10.37	14.83	$t = 2.87, p < .02$
Correctness of Interpretation	11.20	12.82	
Justification for Comments	11.47	14.00	
Desirability of Carter as Roommate	8.89	8.56	
How Strong Recommendation for Carter's Expulsion	16.58	16.11	
How Much Time to Rehabilitate Carter	8.32	9.11	

It should be noted, first, that subjects in the *Hurt* condition judged they had had a much worse effect on Carter's morale than the subjects in the *Help* condition. Their average rating in response to the question "What effect do you feel you had on the morale of the case discussed?" was almost at the lowest end of the scale, where the quantitative verbal designation was "a very bad effect." This would seem to indicate that the experimental manipulation of the subject's seeing himself as having hurt Carter was effective. Damaging Carter's morale, however, did not necessarily imply norm violations. Subjects in the *Hurt* condition may not have felt that they had hurt Carter more than was necessary. On the other hand, spontaneous comments when the experiment was over, as well as the relief shown when it was learned that Carter was a fictitious person, suggest that norm violations were definitely involved for most subjects. Many referred to the charitable interpretations of the second subject as prompting the feeling that they had been overly negative in their approach. Some subjects, of course, were visibly disturbed at what they had done. It is probably safe to infer that, at a minimum, subjects felt embarrassed and ashamed and, at a maximum, profoundly guilty over their conduct.

A second finding of interest is that subjects in the *Hurt* condition have lower evaluations of themselves as psychologists. The question concerned their fitness for a career in psychology —"How capable do you think you would be as a clinical psychologist or psychiatrist?"—and thus presumably produced a thoughtful self-evaluation. Indeed, the *Hurt*-condition subjects' relatively low evaluations of themselves as psychologists were *not* based on their technical competence in interpreting Carter's case. The table shows that the average subject felt he had been as correct in his interpretation of the case and as justified in his commentary as the subject in the *Help* condition. It seems likely, therefore, that the low self-evaluation is based on the subject's estimate of his own capacity for tact, warmth, understanding, and sympathy. Presumably, norm violations occurred with respect to these "human" values.

It should, finally, be noted that the remarks made by Carter did *not* in any significant degree affect his attractiveness. The subjects in the *Hurt* condition found him no more or less desirable as a roommate, recommended his expulsion no more or less strongly, and committed themselves to no more or less time to help rehabilitate Carter than did subjects in the *Help* condition. Thus, if condemnation and avoidance of Carter is a reflection of defensive self-justification on the part of the subjects in the *Hurt* condition, there is no evidence of such a mechanism in these questionnaire data.

In summary, the questionnaire reactions show that subjects in the *Hurt* condition do feel that they have hurt Carter to a relatively serious degree and do think of themselves as relatively less attractive in terms of various human-relations skills, obligations, and values. These findings are in accord with the theoretical view that violation of internal norms governing human relations necessitates a downward re-evaluation of the self. Concerning resolution of the self-evaluation conflict in the *opposite* direction, the questionnaire data revealed no sign of self-defensiveness.

PERSONAL SELF-EVALUATIONS

Following the questionnaire, subjects were requested to assess their personalities on the grounds that such information would be useful to the research program. The procedure consisted simply in their listing their most positive and most negative traits, habits, abilities, values, and so on. Table 24 gives the results of this procedure. Although subjects in the *Hurt* condition listed fewer favorable traits than subjects in the *Help* condition, the difference misses significance. Perhaps the experimental conditions were too weak to cause a re-evaluation of relatively central personality traits, which are notoriously resistant to change and highly variable from individual to individual. If such were the case, then a sampling of subjects in the *Hurt* condition who thought they had severely damaged Carter's morale (that is, those subjects who rated themselves as having had "a very bad effect"), compared with those who judged their effect to be less severe, should display very low self-evaluations in terms of the personality characteristics listed. Table 25 shows this to be the case despite the small number of cases in each condition. If one assumes that, the more a subject thinks he has hurt Carter, the more severe his violation of various self-relevant norms, then the low self-attractiveness can be interpreted as a downward correction of the existing self-evaluation. However, such an interpretation must be viewed with caution, since it is based on a selected sample of subjects.

TABLE 24
MEAN FREQUENCY OF POSITIVE AND NEGATIVE PERSONALITY TRAITS UNDER HURT AND HELP CONDITIONS

Personal Self-Evaluation	Hurt (N = 19)	Help (N = 18)
Positive Traits	4.78	5.38
Negative Traits	3.21	3.16

TABLE 25
MEAN FREQUENCY OF POSITIVE PERSONALITY TRAITS BY SELECTED SUBJECTS IN THE HURT CONDITION

| Self-Evaluation | Damage to Carter's Morale | |
	Severe (N = 9)	Mild (N = 10)
Mean Number of Positive Personality Traits	3.88	5.60

$t = 2.57, p < .02$

REACTIONS REVEALED IN THE MEMORANDA

The personality-evaluation procedure was followed by a request that subjects write notes in which they could summarize their views of the case and emphasize the points which they now considered to be most salient. The experimenter stressed that, although the memos were addressed to Carter, the latter would not see them until a much later phase of the program. Subjects, he assured, would remain completely anonymous.

On the basis of a sample of memos drawn randomly from the *Hurt* and *Help* conditions, three mutually exclusive and exhaustive categories were defined as follows:

Self-Criticism

Most of the memos in this category are explicitly self-critical. Subjects plainly disavow their "wrong" conduct or are critical of the personality characteristics which they see underlying their conduct. In some cases of implicit self-criticism, subjects hold either that they were too negative in their appraisal of Carter or that they ignored some of his potential virtues.

EXAMPLES:

I didn't want to hurt you. . . . I respect you. . . . I would change. . . .

I should have thought more . . . You've probably changed; you've got potential.

You have courage. I judged too harshly. Your orientation has improved.

Self-Justification

Memos in this category emphasize that the writer dealt properly with Carter. Some writers say that their views about Carter would be the same if they had to express them again. Some subjects self-righteously berate Carter. Essentially these are self-defensive memos.

EXAMPLES:

The traits you exhibited, I would never tolerate.

If I was harsh, that's exactly the way I felt; I can't feel sorry.

You are repulsive and should be removed.

Rationalization

The major emphasis in memos belonging to this category is the denial of responsibility for any dire consequences which Carter may suffer as a result of the therapy session. The subject places the entire blame for his harmful conduct upon external conditions beyond his control. Such rationalizations represent another form of self-defense.

EXAMPLES:

I would like to say that the passage I read was poor. . . . It did not give any good attributes of the person.

From the material presented I do not feel that I can judge fairly. . . . The material was incomplete.

A piece of paper relating information about a person cannot discern the true character of a person.

After the categories were formally defined, the total sample of memos was coded without knowledge of the condition from which each had been drawn. An independent coding showed flat disagreements in four out of thirty-seven cases and one slight disagreement based on the meaning of a term. Thus, the reliability of the measures is represented by an agreement between judges of from 85 to 90 per cent.

Table 26 shows the frequency of the classified memos under the *Hurt* and *Help* conditions.

TABLE 26

CLASSIFICATION OF MEMORANDA WRITTEN UNDER
HURT AND HELP CONDITIONS

Classification of Memos	Hurt (N = 19)	Help (N = 18)
Self-Criticism	3	11
Self-Justification	8	6
Rationalization	8	1
	—	—
	19	18

Over-all χ^2 (2 df) = 10.32, p < .01
Corrective vs. Defensive χ^2 (1 df) = 8.02, p < .01

It is evident that the experimental conditions differ as to the nature of the memos concerning Carter. There are fewer subjects in the *Hurt* condition who indulge in self-criticism and more who write self-justifying or rationalizing notes. This result is apparently the reverse of the questionnaire results already reported. It will be recalled that subjects in the *Hurt* condition rated themselves less able as psychologists (see Table 23) and tended to describe their personalities in less favorable terms. In the memoranda, on the other hand, all but three subjects in this condition are definitely *not* self-critical. They do not believe they were too harsh and unsympathetic; overwhelmingly, they affirm their rightness and claim that Carter got from them what he deserved. To check the question of whether the same subjects showed these opposite trends, the distribution of ratings on ability as a psychologist by subjects in the *Hurt* condition was split at the median. The results of this analysis show that *all* of the individuals who rate themselves poor as potential psychologists (that is, those in the lower half of the distribution) write memos which fall into either the self-justifying or rationalizing categories. Not more than 70 per cent of the individuals in the upper half of the distribution, that is, those who think they would make good psychologists, write memoranda which fall into these categories. Possibly because their self-ratings as potential psychologists were fairly concentrated on the lower end of the scale, this apparent inverse relationship between self-rating as a psychologist and the tendency to write self-critical memos does not attain significance. When the distribution of "psychologist" ratings by subjects from both conditions was divided at the median, there was more clear-cut evidence that individuals who give themselves a poor appraisal as psychologists tend to be the very same individuals who write memos that are self-justifying or rationalizing (χ^2 with 2 df = 7.65, p < .03).

ASSESSMENT

If it is assumed that the self-justifying and rationalizing contents of the memos represent defensive self-evaluations, that is, responses designed to defend the individual against a loss of self-esteem, the question is why the same subject's norm-violating conduct previously produced a *downward* correction in his self-evaluation. An answer is suggested by the observation that the self-evaluation conflict induced by violation of internal and external norms is an "approach-avoidance" type. When one response is made—for instance, a self-devaluation—the opposing tendency toward defending against a loss in self-esteem becomes stronger. Thus, it might be supposed that the temporal pattern of results—first the self-devaluation, then the defensively heightened self-evaluation—is an intrinsic characteristic of the stable equilibrium in which the individual finds himself. However, increased response strength is probably not the only explanation of the self-defensiveness found in the subject's memos. It will be recalled that the questionnaire data revealed no difference between conditions as to the evaluation of Carter. Subjects in the *Hurt* condition found him as undesirable as a potential roommate as subjects in the *Help* condition. To the extent that a negative evaluation of Carter reflects the subject's self-defensiveness, subjects who thought they had hurt Carter were no more defensive than subjects in the *Help* condition. The greater self-defensiveness on the part of the subjects in the *Hurt* condition appears only in the memos. Let us consider some of the possible reasons for this.

One kind of opportunity for self-defensive evaluation is provided by the amount of time the individual has for preparation. The writing of the memos came later in the procedure than the self-evaluation ratings. Subjects who theoretically had a greater need to defend themselves, that is, those under the *Hurt* condition, had more time to organize and express in the memos what, to them, were cogent self-defenses.

More importantly, the nature of the qualitative measure itself provided an opportunity for self-defensiveness. The content of the memo was not prescribed by the experimenter, except in the most general terms. The subject could express himself in detail and could organize his message so that the norm violations were weakened or denied. In contrast, the measures of self-evaluation which were administered earlier in the procedure directed the subject only to evaluate his potential as a psychologist. He could do no artful denying. In short, if the subjects in the *Hurt* condition harbored a greater tendency to defend against a loss in self-esteem, owing to their more severe norm violations, the memo-writing measure provided an excellent opportunity for them to do so.

The experiment shows that Carter's distraught behavior, in the wake of conduct by the subject which presumably caused it, made the subject think less of himself as a psychologist and generated something of a tendency for him to be less self-attractive as a total personality. This evidence of lower self-evaluation among the subjects in the *Hurt* condition appears to be consistent with the theoretical view that a violation of one's own norms causes a lowered self-evaluation. The second major finding of the experiment—that subjects in the *Hurt* condition tended to be *less* self-critical and *more* self-defensive in the content of their memoranda—seems also to be consistent with the view that individuals in a self-evaluation conflict will tend to avoid lowering their self-esteem if there is an opportunity to do so. As suggested above, one assumption which would link this result to the theory is that the unstructured memo gave the subject freedom to develop a defensive stance in the form of self-justification or rationalization.

The evidence, however, is not conclusive, and the theoretical interpretation we have placed upon the data can only be a rough and tentative one. Let us summarize some of the major weaknesses which will have to be dealt with. For one thing, we have assumed that the subject's condemnation of Carter, followed by a charitable evaluation of Carter by the supposed second subject, and followed by—in one experimental condition—Carter's emotional display of having been deeply hurt, created violations of various norms for the subject. We assumed, for instance, that subjects in the *Hurt* condition felt guilty or ashamed over having been overheard denouncing Carter or having been excessively hard on him. But this is an assumption empirically supported by nonsystematic data only: the post-experimental admissions of subjects that they did do wrong and observations that they were visibly ashamed and guilty. We should like more systematic evidence that subjects did, in fact, violate their own norms.

Second, we have assumed that it was the violation of norms which caused subjects in the *Hurt* condition to give themselves a relatively poor rating as potential psychologists. But the question arises whether this apparent decrease in self-evaluation was mediated by the norm violation or whether it was wholly and simply an inference which subjects made about their talent after noting the disastrous effects of their behavior upon Carter. Evidence of a causal tie between the severity of norm violation and self-devaluation is suggested by the predictable positive correlation coefficients between, on the one hand, the subject's rating of how much damage he had done to Carter's morale and, on the other, the rating representing his poor potential as a psychologist. (*Hurt* condition, r = +.24; *Help* condition, r = +.23; combined conditions, r = +.43, p<.01.) It should be noted that the correlation is positive (although not high, due to the restricted range of ratings and the size of sample) in the *Help* condition, where subjects could not infer from their effect on Carter that they would make poor psychologists. Another finding relevant to the effect of norm violation was that, considering the subjects from both experimental conditions, those individuals who felt they had had an extremely bad effect on Carter's morale apparently came to see themselves as very unattractive personalities in terms of the number of positive traits they listed. Being unattractive as a total person, unlike being a poor prospect as a psychologist, would not seem to be directly inferable by the subject from the distressing effects of his behavior on Carter. Still, we would like to see more direct evidence that norm violations which occur in the absence of a defensive opportunity lead to lowered self-attractiveness. Third, we have assumed that the subject's assertions, in his memo, of being right, his strong condemnations of Carter, and his blaming the denunciation of Carter on the one-sided case history are, at least in part, examples of self-defensiveness. We should like more direct evidence that such behavior fits the criterion of being defensive. Finally, the greater tendency to write self-justifying and rationalizing memos was assumed to be caused by the greater opportunity for defensiveness inherent in the loose, nondirected form of measurement. To be conclusive about the effect of opportunity, however, this variable ought to be experimentally manipulated.

The following chapter deals with a second experiment on the self-evaluation conflict, which was designed with these problems in mind.

9 The Outcome of a Self-Evaluation Conflict

According to the analysis developed in the preceding chapter, an individual's self-evaluation is affected by his violation of internalized, self-relevant norms. It was proposed that such norm-violating conduct arouses a validation motive which generates a tendency toward lowering the self-evaluation in order to validate the cognitive structure of the self. In turn, the self-devaluation tendency arouses a self-esteem motive which resists such devaluation. In general, then, how norm-violating conduct affects the individual's self-evaluation depends upon the direction in which the evaluation conflict is resolved. Experimental data make it plausible to suppose that the outcome of the conflict depends not only upon the degree of norm violation—stronger violations are less easily defended against—but upon the avail-

160

ability of objective resources in the individual's physical and social environment. If opportunities exist, the individual will tend to seize them and successfully defend against the threat of a loss in self-esteem which the norm violation has generated. In the absence of opportunity for defense, the individual tends to lower his self-evaluation, reflecting a downward correction demanded by the need for a valid cognitive structure. Since what is predicted to happen to the individual's self-evaluation depends on the presence or absence of a defensive opportunity, it is necessary to define the concepts of opportunity and defense in greater detail.

In the pilot experiment previously reported, an opportunity for defense was presumably provided by the unstructured character of a memorandum in which the subject could review his conduct and state his position with the least amount of detriment to himself. There are other kinds of defensive opportunities in everyday life. For example, it is common to observe an individual justify norm-violating conduct on the grounds that others are engaging or have engaged in the same kind of behavior. Perhaps an even more commonly observed basis for self-defense is the citation of authority. If experts implicitly or explicitly support the norm-violating conduct, the individual will use this fact to justify his actions. There are, of course, a number of specific ways in which the perception of others' norm-violating conduct or of supporting opinion by an expert may enable the individual to achieve a self-defense. Social environments may permit the individual to perceive and interpret his norm-violating conduct as not norm-violating, may lead him to see himself as no longer bound by the norm which he has violated, or may produce other kinds of defensive reorganizations.

In any event, given a defensive opportunity, the occurrence of a self-defense can only be inferred from various attitudes and actions observed in norm-violating situations; the attitudes and actions themselves do not necessarily imply defensiveness. For example, in a situation where he severely and excessively condemns another person, the individual can assert that his actions were not really harmful or that the person he hurt deserved it, and so on. Although these self-justifying expressions appear to be defensive, they may be honest and realistic statements of the individual's position without filling any defensive function whatever. Indeed, behavior can properly be called defensive if and only if it is observed to vary with conditions which theoretically should produce defensive behavior *and* if it fulfills the theoretical function of defense, that is, results in a less negative self-evaluation.

An experiment was designed so that we could check specific predictions concerning the direction in which a self-evaluation conflict is resolved. The predictions are based on the hypothesis that the subject's self-evaluation is a function of two conceptually distinct conditions: the severity of norm violation and the availability of a defensive opportunity in the form of expert opinion.

> 1. Holding the availability of defensive opportunity constant, the more severe the norm violation, the more frequent the adoption of self-corrective attitudes— attitudes which theoretically reflect the tendency to lower the self-evaluation to a more valid level.
>
> 2. Holding the severity of the norm violation constant, the greater the defensive opportunity, the more frequent the adoption of self-justifying attitudes— attitudes which theoretically reflect the tendency to defend the self against a loss of self-esteem.

PROCEDURE AND MEASURES

A total of ninety-eight volunteer male subjects, recruited from several undergraduate courses, were run individually in hour-long experimental sessions. Twenty of these subjects were eliminated before analyzing the data because they gave evidence during and after the procedures that they knew they were participating in an experiment. The experiment was conducted in the guise of a survey sponsored by a fictitious "College Disciplinary Committee." The experimenter introduced himself as the assistant secretary to the Committee and directed the subject to be seated at a table in the Committee office. In two of the three experimental conditions, another student—actually a confederate —sat to one side and slightly behind the subject. After the experimenter explained that the Committee was participating in a nationwide survey concerned with problems of student discipline, the subject was presented with a written transcript of a case recently heard by the Committee. It was explained that the transcript was taken from a preliminary hearing and that the final decision as to the defendant's punishment would not be made until the fall meeting of the Committee. Relevant excerpts of the transcript which the subject read are as follows:

> The case before us today is that of Walter B. The defendant has been charged by the dean of the college with a serious offense. I will relate to you what Dean Y. told me about this offense.
>
> Early in March, Dr. R. of the biology department reported to Dean Y. that the scoring key for the California Assessment Examination, Series D, was missing and that he feared some student may have taken it. . . . You may recall that a preliminary investigation threw some suspicion on Walter B., who is a biology major. However, he firmly denied having taken the key and said that he had not known the key was missing. He did say he had some general suspicions about another student—Martin M.—and that he saw Martin examining something that might be the key. Under the circumstances, Martin's room was searched, and the key was found beneath some papers in his desk drawer. You will recall that Martin was immediately suspended from school for the remainder of the semester. This action denied Martin, an outstanding student, the privilege of graduating with his class and seriously jeopardized his chances of being accepted into a graduate school. The effect of the penalty was quite severe and unexpected. You are all aware that Martin has suffered an extreme emo-

tional breakdown and has been under a psychiatrist's
care since the incident. The reactions of Martin to this
penalty, coupled with a number of unexplained circumstances surrounding the theft of the scoring key,
led Dean Y. to continue his investigation of the case.
Suffice it to say that Walter eventually confessed that
he had stolen the scoring key and that, when suspicion fell on him, he "planted" the key in Martin's
desk.

Next reported in the transcript was background information
given by Walter's fraternity president to the effect that Walter
had religious prejudices, was personally unclean, and thought
he was intellectually superior. Finally, it was reported that
Walter had been suspended for plagiarism for three weeks during his sophomore year.

After reading the transcript, the subject was asked to evaluate Walter's personality. He was then requested to indicate
whether or not Walter should be expelled or suspended from
college. His final recommendation on suspension or expulsion
was made after the following experimental conditions were
established.

MILD NORM VIOLATION

It was felt that, to produce a mild norm violation, it
would be necessary to get subjects to denounce Walter's character and to recommend, at least, that he be suspended from
college. It was assumed that such conduct alone would cause
subjects to believe they had been excessively punitive. Although
Walter's conduct was reprehensible, the far-reaching implications of expulsion or even suspension from college would occur
to the subjects as they pondered the issue. In some cases, for
example, their criticism of Walter's character might cause subjects to feel hostility in themselves which they were not aware of
and, thus, might introduce the possibility of bias in their recommendations of expulsion or suspension. Doubts about the punishment fitting the crime could also be stimulated by the thought

that Walter was emotionally sick and thus not fully responsible for his conduct, unconscionable though it may have been. Even though there was no manipulation explicitly aimed at creating norm violations, it seems accurate to assume that the conduct of most subjects would be enough to produce at least a mild violation. It is understood, of course, that some subjects may not have felt they did anything wrong or excessive whatsoever.

SEVERE NORM VIOLATION

In the other two conditions, an attempt was made to create severe norm violations for the subject. First, it was revealed that the defendant—Walter—was present and had heard himself being denounced and his punishment being recommended. Second, the defendant dramatically demonstrated how he had been hurt by the subject. Specifically, after reaching a preliminary decision to recommend expulsion or suspension, the subject was told that Walter was present on the advice of his psychiatrist, who felt that he should hear the opinions of other students. Walter was then given the opportunity to comment before a general discussion was to begin. Visibly shaken, Walter proceeded as follows:

> I don't really think you realize just what you've done here with your judgment for my expulsion [or suspension]. I mean, with your judgments, which the Committee will look at after the summer, my chances for staying in school are just about shot. . . . They'll expel [or suspend] me, and, in my case, that's just about the worst thing that can happen, because my father said this was my last chance. If I'm kicked out of this school, he's not even going to let me go to any other school. So I've had it for any schooling. I mean . . . I know I've done wrong things, which you read on that transcript there . . . even though they're exaggerated there. But a lot of that was because of my drinking, and I've faced that problem. You heard I'm under therapy, and I've been under therapy . . .

and they said I was coming along pretty good there,
and I thought I was doing pretty good myself . . .
until this. . . .

Walter became progressively more pained and upset during his
comments until, shattered, he left the room. Surprised at the
turn of events, the experimenter followed him from the room
but returned alone. After a few moments of vacillation and con-
fusion, the experimenter decided that the session would have to
continue. At this point, the effect of the attempt to create norm
violations was measured.

DEFENSIVE OPPORTUNITY

The opportunity for making a defensive self-evaluation
was introduced after the norm violations had been measured.
It consisted of a letter from Walter's psychiatrist, which was read
into the record by the experimenter.

The conclusion I have drawn from my sessions with
Walter is that he is only superficially disturbed emotionally. He quite frequently acts as if he were disturbed. . . . that is, he unconsciously pretends to be
more sick than he is, and, in so doing, he often lies
compulsively. He plays on the emotions of other
people to gain sympathy. I will say further that Walter
is not making the effort required to curb his impulsive
and childish behavior.

Following the letter (or Walter's exit, in the condition
which did not make a defensive opportunity available), there
was a check on whether the opportunity was recognized by the
subjects.

Measured next was the direction in which the assumed
self-evaluation conflict was resolved: whether the subject adopted
defensive attitudes, that is, attempted to justify his conduct or
adopted self-corrective, self-critical attitudes. A final step in
the procedure was the measurement of the subject's self-evalua-

tion. Each subject was given an open-ended form and requested to list his positive and negative character and personality traits. These data on the subject's self-evaluation made it possible to check on the predicted direction of the conflict resolution.

At the conclusion of the session, the true purpose of the experiment and the rationale for the dissimulation were carefully explained to each subject.

EVIDENCE ON THE VIOLATION OF NORMS

The precondition for the subject's feeling that he had committed at least a mild violation of one or more norms was that he condemned Walter and went on record as recommending punitive action against him. Most subjects did, in fact, do this. All but one subject in each condition explicitly condemned Walter's character, and only two subjects in the entire sample initially and finally recommended punishment less severe than suspension from college.

As to the differential effect of the *Mild-Violation* and *Severe-Violation* conditions, each subject, "in the interests of time and the systematic summary of the discussion," was given a list of eight statements and requested to choose the one which most closely expressed his own attitudes concerning the effect of his conduct on Walter. The statements were:

1. I feel guilty over the thought that I may have hurt the student with some of my remarks.

2. The thought that I may have harmed the student bothers me, and I feel uncomfortable.

3. I feel nervous and upset but cannot identify the reason.

4. I feel somewhat ashamed over my performance.

5. I have a sense of satisfaction over having done a fair and competent job.

6. I feel calm and collected, with no sense of disturbance whatever.

7. I feel angry at the student.

8. I feel full of compassion for the student.

The list was precategorized for the purpose of getting a relatively clear measure of the subject's feeling that he had been wrong in his treatment of Walter. The measure of norm violation was based upon the emotional state reported by the subject. The first four statements represent emotions associated with norm violations. Selection of one or more statements from this category indicates, at a minimum, that the subject was disturbed over the effect he had on Walter and, at a maximum, that he felt guilty over his conduct. Statements 5 and 6 represent emotions associated with norm compliance; certainly no violation is indicated. The last two statements represent emotions directed toward Walter with no reference to the subject's own conduct. They are not directly relevant to norm violation. Table 27 shows the categories from which subjects under the *Mild-Violation* and *Severe-Violation* conditions select their statements.

TABLE 27

REACTIONS OF SUBJECTS TO THEIR CONDUCT TOWARD WALTER
UNDER MILD- AND SEVERE-VIOLATION CONDITIONS

Experimental Condition	Disturbing Emotions	No Disturbance or Self-Satisfaction	Irrelevant to Own Conduct
Mild Violation (N = 26)	3	19	4
Severe Violation (N = 52)	30	15	7

χ^2 (2 df) Over-all = 16.96, p < .001
χ^2 (1 df) Disturbing Emotions vs. No Disturbance = 16.47, p < .001

The number of subjects who consider their conduct to be norm-violating is clearly much larger in the *Severe-Violation* condition. On the other hand, only a small proportion of subjects under the *Mild-Violation* condition select a statement from this category. The difference between conditions in the distribution of subjects is a strong and reliable one whether or not one takes account of the two irrelevant selections. It seems fair to conclude that the conditions which attempted to bring about different degrees of norm violation in the subjects did, in fact, do so.

DEFENSIVE OPPORTUNITY

In essence, the defensive opportunity made available to the subject consisted of information from an authoritative source as to whether or not Walter was emotionally sick. The question is whether this information was actually accepted by the subject. A check on this question was based upon the subject's selection of one of two statements to characterize his own views on Walter's emotional health.

1. I believe the student is not deeply disturbed emotionally and is not sincerely trying to meet and solve his personal problems.

2. I believe the student is deeply disturbed emotionally and is sincerely trying to meet and solve his personal problems.

TABLE 28

NUMBER OF SUBJECTS WHO REGARD WALTER AS SICK UNDER THE
OPPORTUNITY AND NO-OPPORTUNITY CONDITIONS

Experimental Condition	*Walter Sick*	*Walter Not Sick*
Defensive Opportunity (Mild Violation) (N = 26)	10	16
Defensive Opportunity (Severe Violation) (N = 26)	11	15
No Defensive Opportunity (Severe Violation)* (N = 25)	22	3

$$\chi^2 \ (2 \ df) = 15.46, \ p < .001$$

* One subject did not respond.

Table 28 shows that relatively more subjects who were presented with an opportunity for self-defense see Walter as not sick than do subjects who were not given the opportunity.

The evidence can be most clearly seen when the severity of the norm violation is held constant. Without the opportunity made available by the psychiatrist's letter, the overwhelming majority of subjects under the *Severe-Violation* condition look on Walter as being emotionally sick. More than half the subjects under the *Severe-Violation* condition who were presented with the defensive opportunity, on the other hand, stated that they did not believe Walter was sick. There are exceptions to the expected pattern, of course. A few subjects who were not afforded the defensive opportunity maintained that Walter was not sick, and a number of subjects who heard the letter did regard Walter as sick. The relatively large number of subjects in the latter category is probably due to the fact that Walter's behavior in the experimental situation, as well as that described in the case history, did tend to reflect a sick personality.

SELF-JUSTIFYING VERSUS SELF-CORRECTIVE ATTITUDES

On the list from which the subject was requested to choose, there were three classes of statements representing reactions to the self-evaluation conflict induced by norm violation. There was no limitation as to the number of selections within categories and no strict limitation as to how many categories the subject could choose from. The self-corrective statements, which reflect a tendency in the direction of cognitive validation, include various forms of apologies, implied self-criticism, and explicit self-devaluation. The self-justifying category, which reflects a resolution in favor of the self-esteem motivation, includes statements which explicitly condemn Walter or reject the need for apology. A third category represents a self-equivocating attitude, in the sense that the statements have both self-justifying and self-corrective components. It may be assumed that the selection of self-equivocating statements reflects the severity of the norm violation or the difficulty in resolving the self-evaluation conflict which the violation has led to. The complete list of classified statements is as follows:

Self-Corrective

1. I am sorry I made negative judgments about the student; they are likely to have harmful consequences, and I wish there was something I could do to help him.

2. I am sorry for the negative judgments I made about the student; they were wrong. I guess I'm not a very good judge of human nature.

3. I am sorry for the negative judgments I made about the student, as they may have harmful consequences.

4. I guess I was wrong in saying some of the things I did about the student.

Self-Justifying

1. I have concluded that the student is of low moral character; this is evident from the record.

2. I believe the student ought to try to improve his moral and ethical attitudes.

3. I am not sorry for any negative judgments that I made; the student deserved them. I have confidence in my judgments.

4. The student's conduct was so despicable that I feel like denouncing him in the strongest possible terms.

Self-Equivocating

1. I guess I was overly blunt, but the student deserves criticism.

2. My judgments were a bit too harsh, but I only had negative information to go on.

3. I may have been too negative in my judgments, but what I said will probably make very little difference in the final outcome.

4. I may have been too negative, but I'm sure the student will profit by it in the long run.

Table 29 contains the distribution of statements selected from the three categories under each of the experimental conditions.

TABLE 29

PER CENT SELF-JUSTIFYING, SELF-CORRECTIVE, AND SELF-EQUIVOCATING STATEMENTS SELECTED UNDER EXPERIMENTAL CONDITIONS

	Self-Justifying	Self-Corrective	Self-Equivocating	Total Selections
Mild Violation-Defensive Opportunity ($N = 26$)	78%	6%	16%	62
Severe Violation-Defensive Opportunity ($N = 26$)	56	15	29	65
Severe Violation-No Defensive Opportunity ($N = 26$)	49	21	30	65

Mild Viol.-Opp. vs. Severe Viol.-Opp. CR† = 3.14, p < .001*
Severe Viol.-Opp. vs. Severe Viol.-No Opp. CR NS
Mild Viol.-No. Opp. vs. Severe Viol.-No Opp. CR = 3.62, p < .001*

† Critical ratio.
* One-tailed tests.

First, it appears that, when a subject has committed a mild violation, it is easy to resolve the resulting self-evaluation conflict. Only 16 per cent of the statements fall in the self-equivocating category, whereas under the *Severe-Violation* conditions, almost double that percentage of statements are of this type.

Not only is it easier to attempt a resolution in the *Mild-Violation–Opportunity* condition, but the subject can avoid selecting self-corrective statements and readily select self-justifying ones. As the severity of the violation increases, self-justifying attitudes decline in frequency and, when the defensive opportunity (the psychiatrist's letter) is not presented, there is a further decline.

The measure of the number of statements chosen from each category involves more than one selection per individual. An alternate and perhaps more accurate appraisal of the effect of the experimental conditions on the individual is based on the number of subjects who select statements from given categories. An examination of these data shows that *no* subject selects only from the self-equivocating category. This type of statement is selected along with either or both of the two other types. Thus, there are three theoretically relevant categories: 1) the choice of self-justifying statements exclusively or with self-equivocating statements, 2) the choice of self-corrective statements exclusively or with self-equivocating ones, and 3) the selection of both self-justifying and self-corrective statements with, in some cases, self-equivocating ones. A fourth category represents no selection at all. Table 30 shows the distribution of the subjects over these categories.

Under conditions of *Severe Violation,* more subjects adopt both self-justifying and self-corrective attitudes. Such oscillation presumably reflects the severity of the violation felt by the subject. The defensive-opportunity condition, it should be noted, has no effect on this self-equivocation measure. As for the direction of the resolution, with an increase in the severity of the violation, there is a decrease in the number of subjects who select self-justifying statements. When there is no defensive opportunity available, there is a further, significant decrease. Correspondingly, with an increase in the severity of norm violation and in the absence of a defensive opportunity, the number of subjects who choose self-corrective statements goes up.

Since the differences between the mild and severe norm-violation conditions (and between the Defensive-Opportunity–No-Defensive-Opportunity conditions, as measured by the percentage of statements selected, Table 29) are, at best, of borderline significance, two internal analyses were carried out. In the first analysis, two "pure" subgroups were selected. One consisted of subjects who reacted to their conduct toward Walter with un-

TABLE 30

NUMBER OF SUBJECTS WHO SELECT SELF-JUSTIFYING OR SELF-
CORRECTIVE OR BOTH TYPES OF STATEMENTS UNDER
THE EXPERIMENTAL CONDITIONS

	Self-Justifying*	Self-Corrective*	Self-Justifying and Corrective*	No Choices
Mild Violation-Defensive Opportunity (N = 26)	19	0	4	3
Severe Violation-Defensive Opportunity (N = 26)	16	2	7	1
Severe Violation-No Defensive Opportunity (N = 26)	12	7	6	1

Over-all Distribution	χ^2(6 df) = 12.82, p < .05
Self-Justify. vs. Self-Correct.	χ^2(2 df) = 9.90, p < .01
Mild Viol.- Opp. vs. Severe Viol.- Opp.	χ^2(1 df) = 2.10, p < .08†
Severe Viol.- Opp. vs. Severe Viol.- No Opp.	χ^2(1 df) = 3.46, p < .04†

* Includes subjects who additionally chose from self-equivocating category.
† One-tailed tests.

equivocal emotions of guilt, shame, and nervous upset, and the other consisted of subjects who displayed, for example, satisfaction over having done a good job. Then the number of subjects in each of these subsamples who adopted self-justifying attitudes was compared with the number who adopted self-corrective attitudes. The proportion of pure norm violators who adopt self-corrective attitudes greatly exceeds the proportion of norm compliers who do so, and the proportion of the norm compliers who adopt self-justifying attitudes greatly exceeds the proportion of norm violators who do so (χ^2 [1 df] = 7.40, p < .01).

In the second internal analysis, we again compared two selected subgroups: subjects who regarded Walter as not sick (subjects, in other words, who perceived a defensive opportunity) and subjects who recognized that Walter did have emotional problems. A larger proportion of the latter subgroup adopted self-corrective attitudes, and a larger proportion of the subjects who thought that Walter was not sick adopted self-justifying attitudes (χ^2 [1 df] = 8.90, p < .01).

Although we are dealing with selected subjects in these analyses, the results are consistent with those based upon a comparison of the experimental conditions and, thus, suggest that we have essentially intensified the effects of the norm violation and the defensive opportunity.

Considering the data presented in Table 30, it may be objected that the inclusion of subjects who select self-equivocating statements along with either of the other types results in an impure measure of the experimental effects on the adoption of self-justifying and self-corrective attitudes. Accordingly, we may look at the number of subjects who choose statements from the self-justifying category exclusively. Such an analysis shows a steady decrease from 50 per cent in the *Mild-Violation* condition to 35 per cent in the *Severe-Violation* condition to 15 per cent in the *Severe-Violation* condition without the defensive opportunity. Although the number of subjects involved in this analysis is considerably reduced, the differences between each pair of conditions representing the experimental variables approach statistical significance (p < .07), employing one-tailed tests.

DEFENSIVE SELF-EVALUATION

Theoretically, the function of self-justifying attitudes was defensive, in that they helped to avoid a loss in the self-esteem which was threatened by self-corrective tendencies. To prove, however, that such attitudes did, in fact, function as defensive self-evaluations, it is necessary to show that subjects who justified their conduct regarded themselves as more attractive than subjects who selected self-corrective statements did. By the same token, those who did not defend themselves and adopted a self-corrective attitude should have regarded themselves as less personally attractive.

Table 31 presents the mean number of positive and negative personality traits attributed to themselves by subjects who selected self-justifying or self-corrective statements.

TABLE 31

MEAN NUMBER OF POSITIVE AND NEGATIVE PERSONALITY TRAITS
ATTRIBUTED TO THEMSELVES BY SUBJECTS WHO SELECT
SELF-JUSTIFYING OR SELF-CORRECTIVE STATEMENTS

Self-Evaluation	Self-Justifying* (N=46)	Self-Corrective* (N=9)	Both* (N=17)	No Choice (N=4)
Positive	4.30‡	4.78	3.82	7.00‡
Negative	2.74†	3.78†	2.76	3.75

* Includes subjects who also select self-equivocating statements.
‡ Difference between these means t = 2.54, p < .02.
† Difference between these means t = 2.04, p < .05.

Concerning the theoretical derivation, it should be noted that the subjects who adopt self-justifying attitudes list significantly fewer negative traits—are more attractive to themselves as personalities—than subjects who adopt self-corrective attitudes. A second, unexpected finding is that subjects who do not choose from any category (despite the small sample size) list a larger number of positive traits than those who select self-justifying statements.

The fact that subjects who adopt self-justifying attitudes are more attractive to themselves than are subjects who adopt self-corrective attitudes would appear to confirm the deduction that self-evaluation is a function of the resolution of a conflict about the self. At the same time, it confirms the assumption that self-justifying attitudes do function as a self-defense which enables the subject to avoid self-devaluation. However, this analysis is based upon selected subjects, culled from the three experimental conditions according to the types of statements they chose. It is quite possible, consequently, that subjects who select self-justifying statements are characteristically less negative about themselves than subjects who choose self-corrective statements. In other words, rather than self-evaluation being a function of the relative amount of self-defensiveness, which, in turn, is determined by the experimental conditions, the subject's basic personality may be responsible, wholly independently of the experimental conditions.

Such an argument, however, must contend with the fact that subjects who adopt self-justifying attitudes *do* differ across experimental conditions in ways relevant to the predicted effects of the conditions. For instance, there are significant differences across conditions in the relative number of self-justifying and self-corrective subjects who feel guilty, ashamed, or disturbed over their conduct toward Walter. Since these subjects are differentially affected by the experimental conditions, it is plausible to assume they do not comprise a homogeneous sample of personalities. In other words, it can be more readily assumed that self-evaluation was a result of the conflict resolution than of a personality tendency.

If it is not a chance event, the finding that those who make neither self-justifying nor self-corrective choices list a significantly greater number of positive traits for themselves than those who do select self-justifying statements raises an intriguing possibility. If the no-choice subjects can be regarded as those who tend to "withdraw" from a norm-violation–induced-self-evaluation conflict, the suggestion is that such a withdrawal has the effect of creating, or is associated with, a different kind of defense— namely, the illusion of superiority.

ASSESSMENT

The results lend at least modest support to the general hypothesis that self-evaluation is a function of the direction in which a norm-violation–induced conflict is resolved. The results also support the specific hypotheses concerning the effects of the severity of norm violation and the existence of defensive opportunity upon the direction of conflict resolution. The hypothesized chain of events, however, is rather long and complex; it should be examined carefully for weak links and for possibilities of simplification.

Although there was evidence that norm violations were

committed,[1] the evidence that a self-evaluation conflict was induced by the violation is wholly inferential, based on the differential pattern of attitudes adopted across experimental conditions. It would tighten and simplify the theoretical argument if the self-evaluation conflict were induced directly rather than by way of norm-violation procedure.

It is tempting to place an interpretation on the data without reference to the hypothesized self-evaluation conflict and its resolution. Thus, the greater his norm violation, the more the subject regrets his conduct, as indicated by the more frequent instances of what have been called self-corrective attitudes. Regret is a superficial emotion which is often used instrumentally to placate the person whom one is harming. If regret were the whole story, however, it is unlikely that subjects who showed it would also show rather negative self-evaluations concerning central portions of personality. Such negative self-assessment reflects more than mere regret.

Another interpretation bears on the effect of the defensive-opportunity condition. It might be contended that the letter from the psychiatrist was, in effect, a persuasive communication from a high-status source. Such a social influence caused the subject to change his attitude toward Walter in a negative direction. But this interpretive frame of reference is not entirely satisfactory, either. For although it might account for a change in attitude toward Walter, it would not account for the relatively positive self-evaluation of the subject. Indeed, the psychiatrist's letter, representing the defensive-opportunity con-

---

1. In addition to formal data, there were anecdotal observations which strongly suggested that norm violations had been created. For example, following one exit by Walter in the *Severe-Violation* condition, an obviously disturbed subject ran after him, calling out to him to return and be helped. Several subjects appeared to be stunned, apparently feeling they had done something very wrong. Another possible indication that norm violations had been induced was the greater consumption of water by the subjects in the *Severe-Violation* conditions. Of the subjects who drank at all from a glass which the experimenter had placed on the table, those in the severe conditions consumed an estimated average of .6 of a glass, whereas those in the *Mild-Violation* condition drank an average of .4 of a glass ($t = 2.00$, $p = .05$).

dition, had nothing whatever to do with the *subject's* personality.[2]

Also concerning the interpretation of the defensive-opportunity condition, it could be argued that the psychiatrist's letter had its effect by directly reducing the severity of the norm violation rather than by enabling the subject to make a defensive cognitive reorganization with respect to his norm-violating conduct. In other words, the experimental procedure for inducing the degree of norm violation and the reading of the psychiatrist's letter were merely two ways of manipulating the same factor. The defensive-opportunity condition, however, did not affect the measures of the degree of norm violation (the percentage of self-equivocating statements selected in Table 29 and the number of subjects who selected both types of statements in Table 30).

There is one consideration which does stand formidably in the way of an unequivocal interpretation, however. The cognitive-validation need, by way of its derivative self-corrective tendency, is not the only possible source of lowered self-evaluation. It is possible to assume that at least part of the self-corrective attitude adopted under conditions of norm violation reflects a conditioned self-punishment response. Early in life, the individual learns that transgression of moral standards results in punishment. Through a process of identification, the individual also comes to be an agent of society in accepting and maintaining its moral and ethical codes. Thus, as an individual, he avoids transgression and becomes anxious in the anticipation of it for fear of social punishment. As a social agent, he punishes himself for anticipated or actual transgression. With the development of an internalized society or superego, the individual becomes a self-policed member of society, fearing his own punishment when there might be, or actually is, a transgression. According to this view, the self-corrective attitudes, shown to

2. The effect of the *Defensive-Opportunity* condition appears to be reflected by the fact that subjects who did not hear the psychiatrist's letter reduced the term of suspension from their initial to their final recommendations by twice as much as subjects who did hear the psychiatrist's letter.

increase with the severity of norm violation, might represent guilt reactions based upon the conditioned association between transgression and self-punishment. What is needed is an experimental design which holds constant the operation of the superego need and varies the cognitive-validation need. An experimental design in which this crucial requirement is met is described in the following chapter.

10 The Projection of Unfavorable Personality Characteristics

In the experiment just reported, the individual appeared to lower his self-evaluation so that it matched the more valid estimate of his worth inferred from his norm-violating conduct. If, however, an authoritative opinion made available to him implicitly supported his wrong conduct, the individual was able to avoid the self-devaluation demanded by the self-validation pressure. In essence, such a defensive opportunity allowed the individual to reinterpret his behavior so that it no longer was regarded as an ethical or moral violation.

The self-evaluation conflict resolved through such a defensive reorganization was a comparatively simple one because the self-validation tendency was only in the direction of self-devaluation. It is often the case, however, that self-validation tendencies are themselves in conflict. For instance, if a student who thinks of himself as having high intellectual ability is suddenly given evidence that he is mediocre in some important subject, there is a conflict as to which is his "true" valuation. In such a situation, the opposition of the two valuations, plus the opposition of the unfavorable one to the self-esteem drive, makes for a *double* self-evaluation conflict. A frequently observed process of resolving these complicated conflicts of personality characteristics involves the attribution of the unfavorable characteristic to another person or persons. Such "projection" seems to operate on the general principle that, if others possess a negative characteristic or possess more of it, the characteristic becomes easier to accept in oneself. By comparing himself with others, the individual is no longer uniquely or absolutely unattractive to himself in terms of the unfavorable characteristic. By projection, then, the individual can not only reduce the threat to his self-esteem, but validate his self-evaluation at the same time.

An analysis of self-evaluation conflict as it relates to projection enables us to eliminate a couple of weak links in the chain of argument developed thus far concerning the determinants of self-evaluation. In the previous treatment of the problem, the self-evaluation conflict was based on the violation of various norms of conduct. But such a norm-violating procedure is an indirect way of creating the conflict; the existence of the latter can only be assumed. A second and more important problem is that the observed reactions to norm violation can be derived from conflicting tendencies of a fundamentally different kind from those which compose the kind of self-evaluation conflict we have postulated. Specifically, self-corrective attitudes, consisting of various forms of self-criticism and self-depreciation, can be interpreted as self-punitive responses based on the need to salve the conscience following a moral transgression rather than as the reflection of a self-validation tendency. Self-justifying attitudes, for that matter, can be taken to represent aggressiveness—the id component of a superego conflict—rather than representing a need to maintain self-esteem.

The following analysis of the self-esteem and self-validation determinants of projection is based upon a directly induced self-evaluation conflict. Such an approach not only eliminates the step of getting the individual to violate norms, but provides a strong argument against interpreting changes in self-evaluation as a function of a superego conflict and its attendant dynamics of guilt, self-punishment, and the like. A self-evaluation conflict can be created when an individual who already has a positive self-evaluation in some dimension receives reliable information which is unequivocally negative about this or a related aspect of himself. Theoretically involved, on the one hand, is a pressure on the individual to re-evaluate himself more negatively so as to bring his self-concept into closer correspondence with the reality represented by the unfavorable disclosure. On the other hand, in the absence of complete certainty about the negative information communicated to him, the existing positive self-evaluation may be considered the valid estimate in the given content area. In such circumstances, the individual suffers a conflict based upon mutually contradictory self-validation tendencies. In addition, one can assume that the negative information which is disclosed to the individual is a threat to his self-esteem and gives rise to a unidirectional pressure toward maintaining or enhancing that self-esteem. Considering the structure of this double conflict, it is evident that *both* self-validation and self-esteem needs can be satisfied if the individual can lessen the threat of the newly disclosed negative personality characteristic and thus maintain the existing positive self-evaluation. If the negative information disclosed to him is so reliable that it must be accepted, the individual can be expected to project the unfavorable characteristic to another person or persons. As already suggested, if other persons share the negative characteristic or possess more of it then he himself does, the individual feels the characteristic to be less threatening. For the individual who has a positive self-evaluation, projection not only takes care of the threat to his self-esteem, but obviates the need for the negative re-evaluation of himself demanded by self-validation pressure.

Of course, if the individual who receives the negative information about his personality has a negative self-evaluation to

begin with, there is little or no conflict so far as the self-validation need is concerned. The existing unfavorable self-evaluation
and the evaluation implied by the negative information are
mutually consistent. But the negative disclosure about himself
still threatens to confirm or to lower the individual's already
low self-esteem. Consequently, the tendency to avoid a loss in
self-esteem conflicts with the tendency to affirm the validity of
his existing negative self-evaluation. This is a single conflict
between self-esteem and self-validation, however, in contrast to
the case in which, additionally, self-validation tendencies are
themselves in conflict. Therefore, a reduced tendency to attribute
the negative personality characteristic to another person or persons is to be expected.

A similar two-component analysis can be made of the self-
evaluation conflict created by the communication of reliable
information which is unequivocally favorable to the individual.
In this case, it is the individual with an existing negative self-
evaluation for whom there is a double motivational conflict.
First, he is in a quandary as to which evaluation is valid. Second,
it is probably safe to assume that an individual with a "pre-
existing" low self-evaluation—that is, one which has already been
induced experimentally—does harbor a tendency to enhance
his self-esteem. In such a case, by attributing to another person
or persons at least some of the negative personality characteristics
upon which the existing low self-evaluation is based, the individual can enhance his self-esteem and resolve the validation
conflict at the same time.

For an individual who has a positive self-evaluation to begin with, there is no conflict induced by the favorable disclosure.
That is, the validity of the existing self-evaluation is confirmed
by the reliable and unequivocally positive information he receives, and the self-esteem need does not come into operation
at all.

The foregoing analysis is probably oversimplified as far as
the content of the projection is concerned. What is projected
doesn't have to be exactly the same unfavorable personality
characteristic which the individual is newly informed about or

which already exists in him. Everyday observation suggests that there are all kinds of substitutions possible. Thus, for example, instead of projecting the negative characteristic about which he is newly informed, the individual may project a related negative trait, or he may attribute less of an existing positive personality trait, and so on.

With this qualification in mind, the analysis of self-evaluation conflicts created by the communication of positive and negative information about the individual's personality appears to lead to the prediction of a statistical interaction effect: Given a reliable negative disclosure about the self, those subjects with positive self-evaluations should attribute to another person more of some negative personality characteristic (or less of some positive personality characteristic) than those subjects with negative self-evaluations. On the other hand, given a favorable disclosure about the self, those with existing negative self-evaluations should attribute to another person more of some negative characteristic (or less of some positive characteristic) than those with positive self-evaluations.

It can also be postulated, on intuitive grounds, that the act of attributing one's personal characteristics to someone else presupposes some relationship with that person. If the other person is very different from oneself, it is difficult to conceive that such a person can possess any negative personality characteristic present in oneself. To estimate, for example, that one's partner is extremely hostile—a negative characteristic—is probably quite difficult if the partner belongs to an entirely different culture or, in general, is utterly outside the judgmental framework of the individual. Accordingly, it may be hypothesized that when other persons are similar, the predicted interaction pattern of projection, as a function of disclosure and self-evaluation, will be exaggerated.

An experimental design which would permit a clear test of these hypotheses was based upon Bramel's (1962) ingenious investigation of the projection of homosexuality. Since Bramel's formulation and analysis of the problem in terms of dissonance theory are highly relevant to our own, it will be useful to examine them in some detail.

According to the dissonance approach, the subject's being aroused by viewing pictures of nude males conveys negative information to him about himself, namely, that he has at least latent homosexual inclinations. Strong dissonance, or self-inconsistency, however, is created only for those subjects who have an initially high self-evaluation; there is little or no self-contradiction for those who already have a low self-evaluation. In the normal course of events, the strong dissonance would be reduced by denying the negative information. But when information about the nature of one's sexuality comes from a sensitive and reliable source, in this case, from a psychogalvanic skin response picked up by electrodes and registered on a microammeter, it is not easily turned aside. Projection of the homosexuality acknowledged in oneself is a more feasible mode of dissonance reduction. Thus, for example, if others are at least as homosexual as he is, the individual tends to regard himself as relatively less unattractive. Actually, under certain conditions, Bramel did find evidence of greater projection on the part of subjects in whom a high self-evaluation had been induced than on the part of low self-evaluation subjects. It should be noted that, from the standpoint of psychoanalytic theory, the clash between the superego or conscience and the repressed impulse (homosexuality) was objectively constant; subjects in both conditions of self-evaluation received the same objectionable information about themselves. Consequently, one is not able to explain the projection in terms of guilt anxiety or the superego-id conflict which generates such anxiety.

The question may be raised as to whether the inconsistency of the individual's self-evaluation *alone* determined the projection or whether a defense against loss of self-esteem must also be taken into account. An interpretation based only on dissonance can be compared with our own interpretation in terms of conflicting self-validation and self-esteem motivations. If a condition of self-inconsistency per se is responsible for projection, the manner in which the inconsistency is constituted should, in principle, make no difference in its disturbing effects. That is, an individual with a negative self-evaluation who receives favorable information about himself should experience just as strong a dissonance as the individual with a positive self-evaluation who receives negative information about himself. In both cases, there is a self-contradiction. Secondly, if the function of projection is merely and exclusively to reduce the inconsistency, it should not make any difference whether negative or positive personality characteristics are projected. The inconsistency between having an initially negative self-evaluation and being informed that one is highly positive in some important characteristic could be resolved by the projection of the favorable characteristic, just as the inconsistency between having a positive self-evaluation and receiving negative information about oneself could be reduced by the projection of the unfavorable characteristic. Specifically, for the individual with a negative self-evaluation who is informed that he possesses an unusual amount of masculinity—a highly attractive trait for males—the dissonance could be reduced by his attributing even more masculinity to others, which would leave him relatively less attractive to himself, consistent with his self-evaluation. There is no clearly specified reason in dissonance theory why the projection of masculinity would not take place in order to remove the self-contradiction. If, on the other hand, defense against loss of self-esteem is a determinant of projection, the individual with a negative self-evaluation who receives favorable information about his masculinity should definitely be expected to project less masculinity. According to this view, the attribution to others of less masculinity or of more of some negative personality characteristic, relative to the amount the individual himself possesses, can be interpreted as a defense against loss of self-esteem and a simultaneous resolution of the conflict concerning the validity of the individual's self-evaluation.

In addition to the projection of sexuality, the attribution of a number of personality characteristics was studied for evidence bearing on the interaction hypothesis. Some of these were related to the sexuality characteristic disclosed to the individual; others were the same as or related to the personality traits which comprised the experimentally induced positive and negative self-evaluations.

PROCEDURE AND MEASURES

A total of one hundred and ten male undergraduate volunteers participated in an initial testing period. Of these, eighty also participated in the actual experimental session. The subjects were assigned at random to one of several experimental conditions, based on the combinations of three variables: 1) In each pair, one subject had a high self-evaluation experimentally induced and the other, a low one. 2) For each subject, the partner was represented as either similar or dissimilar in terms of socioeconomic, educational, and other general criteria. 3) In each pair, both members received the same positive or negative information about their sexuality.

The creation of a positive or a negative self-evaluation was based on a battery of personality tests given to the subjects before the experimental session. The battery included a questionnaire actually designed to measure the subject's degree of anxiety in everyday social situations, a projective ink-blot test similar to the Rorschach, and a word-matching test of a familiar type used for psychiatric screening. After completing this material and a biographical questionnaire used to establish the similarity or dissimilarity of the partner, subjects were told they would receive a confidential report of their personality-test results during the second session and that some physiological measures would be taken at that time.

At the beginning of the second session, each subject of a pair was given a detailed report supposedly based on the personality tests that had been taken. At random, one subject was given a favorable report about his personality and the other, an unfavorable one. The negative report covered such general personality dimensions as anger, including hostility toward the self and others in general, immaturity with respect to heterosexual and interpersonal relations, personal inefficiency and disorganization, and social insensitivity. The positive report consisted of favorable aspects of the same general personality dimensions: Subjects were told that they harbored little hostility and that they were highly mature, efficient, and socially sensitive. Following the induction of a positive or negative self-evaluation in this manner, each subject filled out a self-evaluation form. This consisted of fifteen personality traits which could be evaluated in either a negative or a positive direction on a 7-point scale. The subject was asked to rate the degree to which each trait characterized him.

After this procedure, each subject was asked to step out of his booth and describe to his partner any play, motion picture, or book he had recently seen or read. The purpose of this face-to-face contact was to provide a realistic retrospective base for the impression of similarity or dissimilarity which was to be manufactured a moment later. Their brief descriptive comments finished, the subjects were again seated in separate booths, and each was given a biographical sheet that the other had supposedly filled out. Actually, what was presented to the subject was a falsified form which showed the same or a different pattern of responses in terms of fraternity membership, occupation of father, educational aspirations, and similar categories. When the subject had compared his biographical form with that of the other subject, he filled in a 7-point check list which indicated how similar or dissimilar he thought his partner was to himself.

Both subjects were then told that the main topic being studied was basic sexuality. It was said that traditional methods, such as those employed by Kinsey, were rather unreliable and of questionable validity; recent physiological measures were far more sensitive and dependable. Given at this point was a detailed explanation of the psychogalvanic skin response and its use in the measure of emotional arousal states. It was explained to each subject that the sensitive electrodes which had been attached to his hand would detect his level of sexual arousal and register it on the highly reliable microammeter on the small table in front of him.

Pairs of subjects in the *Positive-Disclosure* condition were told they would be shown pictures of females in various stages of undress. They were told with careful and convincing technical elaboration that a high dial reading would indicate basic virility. In the *Negative-Disclosure* condition, other pairs of subjects were told they would see males in various stages of undress and, with a technically convincing rationale, that a high dial reading would indicate latent homosexuality.

To establish the *Negative-Disclosure* condition, the pairs of subjects were shown fifteen pictures of males. These were cut out of physical-culture and art magazines and ranged from fully clothed to completely nude. To establish the *Positive-Disclosure* condition, the pairs of subjects were shown fifteen female pictures. These also ranged from fully clothed to completely nude. The two series were carefully matched in terms of physical attractiveness, pose, and amount of skin exposure. In both conditions, the procedure was the same: The pictures were presented one at a time and exposed for ten seconds in a box which could be seen by both subjects. Wires from the microammeter in each booth led to a control panel. Here, according to a predetermined schedule which was constant for both disclosure conditions, an assistant created identical needle deflections for both subjects during the exposure of each picture. The electrodes on the subjects' hands were, of course, dummies. For most of the fifteen pictures, the microammeter values were in the upper ranges of the 0–100–degree scale, indicating either a highly homosexual response, in the case of the *Negative-Disclosure* condition, or a highly virile response, in the *Positive-Disclosure* condition.

On each of the fifteen trials, the subject recorded his own galvanic skin response (GSR) which he read on the 100-unit scale and estimated his partner's reading on the same scale. The score respresenting the projection of homosexuality and masculinity was the sum, over the fifteen trials, of the differences between the the dial reading he was given experimentally, and the dial reading he estimated for his partner. For both disclosure conditions, the more positive this summed discrepancy—that is, the higher the estimate of the partner's sexuality (homosexuality or masculinity in the *Negative-Disclosure* or *Positive-Disclosure* conditions respectively)—the greater the amount of projection.

Following the GSR procedure, the subjects were given a list of various personality characteristics relevant to the induced self-evaluation or to the disclosure of latent homosexuality or virility. Specifically, the subject had to rate himself and his partner on each of ten emotional states. The states were: sexual arousal, vague pleasure, nervousness, shame, fear, anger toward self, anger toward experimenter, generalized anger, moral disgust, and physical disgust. The ratings on each emotional characteristic were made on a 7-point scale labeled "Not at All" on the low end and "Very Strongly" on the high. The measure of projection of any of these emotional characteristics was based on the difference between the subject's self-rating and his rating of his partner. As in the case of sexuality, the more positive this discrepancy, the greater the projection of the given characteristic.

When this procedure was finished, subjects were asked to rate the favorability of the information they had received from the dial readings. A 7-point scale was used to determine whether *Positive-* and *Negative-Disclosure* conditions communicated the appropriate implications for personality. The scale ranged from "Very Favorable" through "Neutral" to "Very Unfavorable."

The experiment finished, the subjects were given a complete explanation of the purposes and procedures, along with a brief statement on the normality and abnormality of heterosexuality and homosexuality. Considerable care was taken to deal with any discernible anxiety that had been aroused. The vast majority of the subjects reported that they enjoyed their participation in the experiment.

SELF-EVALUATION, PARTNER SIMILARITY, AND INFORMATION DISCLOSURE

Table 32 contains evidence that the procedures for inducing the three experimental conditions were entirely successful in their effects. The average over-all self-evaluation rating, based on the fifteen positive- and negative-personality-trait scales, is higher for subjects in the *Positive Self-Evaluation* condition than for subjects in the *Negative Self-Evaluation* condition. The *Similar-Dissimilar* treatment also seems to have been effective in terms of the subjects' ratings on the 7-point scale used to measure this variable. Finally, subjects who were exposed to the fifteen female pictures rated the personality implications of their reaction to the pictures as more favorable than did subjects who were exposed to the male pictures. This shows that the information conveyed to the subjects implied a positive or negative personality characteristic, as intended. The experimental conditions, then, were successfully induced.

TABLE 32

MEAN RATINGS OF SELF-EVALUATION, SIMILARITY OF PARTNER,
AND FAVORABILITY OF DISCLOSURE UNDER
EXPERIMENTAL CONDITIONS

Experimental Conditions	*Self-Evaluation Rating*	
Positive Self-Evaluation	77.23	
		t=2.13, p<.05
Negative Self-Evaluation	72.73	
	*Rating of Partner's Similarity**	
Similar	4.85	
		t=6.12, p<.01
Dissimilar	3.38	
	Rating on Favorability of Information†	
Positive Disclosure (Female Pictures)	4.47	
Negative Disclosure		t=3.50, p<.01
(Male Pictures)	3.81	

* Higher scores indicate greater similarity.
† Higher scores indicate more favorable implications.

PROJECTION OF MASCULINITY
AND HOMOSEXUALITY

It will be recalled that, the more the positive discrepancy, the more the projection; the more the negative discrepancy, the less the projection. In Table 33, the mean projection scores are grouped under the experimental conditions in which they were obtained.

TABLE 33

MEAN PROJECTION OF MASCULINITY AND HOMOSEXUALITY
UNDER THREE EXPERIMENTAL CONDITIONS

	Negative Disclosure (Male Pictures)		Positive Disclosure (Female Pictures)	
Initial Self-Evaluation	*Similar*	*Dissimilar*	*Similar*	*Dissimilar*
Positive	− 2.8	− 2.4	− 0.1	− 0.1
Negative	− 2.0	− 3.0	+ 1.6	− 0.7
Difference between Disclosure conditions			$F = 11.00, p < .01$	
Difference between Self-Evaluation conditions			NS	
Difference between Similarity conditions			NS	
Interaction of Self-Evaluation and Disclosure			NS	

An analysis of variance shows that the amount of projection differs only between the disclosure conditions. Subjects who were exposed to the male pictures project less homosexuality than the counterpart group of subjects, exposed to the female pictures, project masculinity. There are two interpretive points that might be made about this rather clear-cut finding. First of all, estimates of the partner's personality characteristics are determined by objective considerations quite apart from the dynamics of defensive projection under investigation. Thus, for subjects in the *Negative-Disclosure* condition, the probability of one's partner being homosexual is low. For subjects in the *Positive-Disclosure* condition, the probability of one's partner being virile is higher. Given that the pairs of subjects in each condition accepted the disclosure that their sexuality was of a high order, one would expect a greater projection of masculinity than of homosexuality on the basis of such probability considerations alone. A second possibility to consider seriously is that the attribution of homosexuality to the partner is much more inhibited than the attribution of masculinity by fear of arousing the ire of the partner.

The similarity of the partner on group-membership criteria appears to have had no effect whatever on the attribution of homosexuality or masculinity to him.

Of major interest theoretically is the *joint* effect of the Disclosure conditions and the Self-Evaluation conditions initially induced in subjects on the amount of projection. It was expected that subjects with positive self-evaluations would project more homosexuality in the *Negative-Disclosure* condition and more masculinity in the *Positive-Disclosure* condition than those who had negative self-evaluations. In other words, the scores representing the projection of homosexuality should be more positive for subjects under the *Positive-Self-Evaluation* condition than for subjects under the *Negative-Self-Evaluation* condition. Scores representing the projection of masculinity should be more negative for subjects under the *Negative-Self-Evaluation* condition than for subjects under the *Positive-Self-Evaluation* condition. Table 33 shows that neither of these predictions, summarized in the interaction term of the analysis of variance, was upheld. We may raise again the speculation that perhaps the rather bald attribution of homosexualty and the relative underattribution of masculinity, predicted on the part of the *Positive-Self-Evaluation* subjects in the *Negative-Disclosure* condition and the *Negative-Self-Evaluation* subjects in the *Positive-Disclosure* condition, gave rise to anxiety which prevented the differential effects of these conditions from showing up. In any case, we must count these results as a failure of the hypothesis as far as the projection of sexuality is concerned.

PROJECTION OF EMOTIONAL CHARACTERISTICS

Let us now turn to the projection of emotional characteristics. The measure of projection of such material is the difference between the subject's rating of himself and, on the same scale, his estimate of his partner with regard to the given characteristic. The larger the positive discrepancy, the greater the projection of the emotional characteristic.

Examination of these data shows that there are differences between the *Disclosure* conditions in the projection of *vague pleasure* (subjects exposed to male pictures project more vague pleasure than subjects exposed to female pictures), *shame* (subjects exposed to male pictures project less shame than subjects exposed to female pictures), and anger toward self (subjects exposed to male pictures project less anger with themselves than subjects exposed to female pictures). Concerning the emotional characteristic of pleasure, one can readily assume that subjects who viewed male pictures would tend to strongly deny, to a greater extent than subjects who viewed pictures of females, that they actually derived pleasure from the experience. Indeed, the latter subjects might be disposed to admit their pleasurable arousal quite openly. Subjects exposed to male pictures should, therefore, tend to rate their partners relatively higher than themselves on pleasurable arousal—in order to reduce subjectively the amount of pleasure they derived—whereas subjects exposed to female pictures should tend to rate their partners as having experienced relatively less pleasure than they did.

In the case of shame and self-directed anger, subjects under the *Positive-Disclosure* condition probably would be inclined to deny such emotional reactions. Individuals who are led to think of themselves as virile almost by definition are unlikely to be ashamed or angry with themselves for having such a befitting personality characteristic. Although they are essentially negative characteristics, shame and self-directed anger would seem to be more appropriate reactions to the disclosure of homosexuality than to the disclosure of virility. Hence, the relatively smaller amount of projection of them by subjects under the *Negative-Disclosure* conditions.

The joint effect of intial self-evaluation and subsequent disclosure on the projection of personality characteristics can be constructed from the data presented in the next two tables. Table 34 shows the amount of shame projected under each of the experimental conditions; Table 35 shows the amount of general hostility or anger under each of the experimental conditions.

Important to note in both tables is that, of the subjects who saw the male pictures, those who have a positive self-evaluation tend to attribute more shame and general anger to the partner relative to the amount attributed to themselves than those who have a negative self-evaluation. Of those subjects who were exposed to the female pictures, the subjects who have a negative

TABLE 34
MEAN PROJECTION OF SHAME

Initial Self-Evaluation	Negative Disclosure (Male Pictures)		Positive Disclosure (Female Pictures)	
	Similar	Dissimilar	Similar	Dissimilar
Positive	− 0.3*	+ 0.3	+ 0.2	0.0
Negative	− 0.2	− 0.4	+ 1.1	+ 0.8

Difference between Disclosure conditions	$F = 9.37, p < .01$
Difference between Self-Evaluation conditions	NS
Difference between Similarity conditions	NS
Interaction of Disclosure and Self-Evaluation	$F = 6.74, p < .05$

* The larger the positive quantity, the greater the projection.

TABLE 35
MEAN PROJECTION OF GENERALIZED ANGER

Initial Self-Evaluation	Negative Disclosure (Male Pictures)		Positive Disclosure (Female Pictures)	
	Similar	Dissimilar	Similar	Dissimilar
Positive	+ 0.2*	+ 0.2	+ 0.2	− 0.1
Negative	− 0.3	0.0	+ 0.6	+ 0.4

Difference between Disclosure conditions	NS
Difference between Self-Evaluation conditions	NS
Difference between Similarity conditions	NS
Interaction of Disclosure and Self-Evaluation	$F = 4.78, p < .05$

* The larger the positive quantity, the greater the projection.

self-evaluation tend to attribute more shame and general anger to the partner relative to the amount they attribute to themselves than subjects who have a positive self-evaluation.

ASSESSMENT

The statistically significant interactions shown in Tables 34 and 35 appear to be in line with theoretical expectations. To summarize the argument briefly: Subjects in whom a positive self-evaluation was initially induced experience a strong conflict about themselves when informed of their homosexuality, a most undesirable personality trait. They not only experience a conflict as to their true worth, but are threatened by a loss of self-esteem, a circumstance which conflicts with the need to avoid such a loss. To resolve the double conflict in a way which both defends their self-esteem and validates their estimates of self-worth, these subjects attribute a relatively larger degree of negative personality characteristics to their partners than do subjects in whom a negative self-evaluation was initially induced. For the latter, the conflict aroused by the negative disclosure is comparatively weak. Although the negative information about themselves does threaten their self-esteem, it also confirms the validity of their existing self-evaluations.

The disclosure of favorable information to subjects, namely, that they are virile personalities, creates a strong conflict for those in whom a negative self-evaluation was induced. For this group, there is a conflict pertaining to the validity of the self-evaluation, in addition to some threat associated with its low self-esteem. To resolve the conflict in a way that avoids further loss of self-esteem and simultaneously validates the self-evaluation, these subjects project more unfavorable personality characteristics than do subjects who initially are led to feel positive about themselves. The latter group presumably has no need for validation and is not threatened by any loss of self-esteem.

The projection of masculinity and homosexuality was, contrary to prediction, unaffected by the self-evaluation and self-disclosure conditions. It has already been suggested that to go on record to the effect that one's partner is homosexual or is deficient in masculinity involved too much risk for the subjects in terms of partner retaliation. These are not allegations designed to promote friendship; certainly, they are more pejorative than the attribution of the somewhat more ambiguous emotional characteristics. Even though a trait like "nervousness" is generally an unfavorable one, the subject who attributes a relatively large quantity of it to another can more easily be pardoned than if he attributes homosexuality. Yet, despite the greater ease of attributing emotional characteristics, only the projection of shame and hostility showed the expected effects of the self-evaluation and disclosure conditions. Why there was no differential projection in the cases of nervousness, vague pleasure, physical and moral disgust, sexual arousal, fear, anger toward self, and anger with experimenter, we do not know. Perhaps inhibition was also associated with some of these emotional characteristics. But, a priori, it is difficult to detect any property which clearly differentiates shame and hostility from the other characteristics. Only further research can give us an understanding of what happened. In general terms, it can be said that the degree to which a negative personality characteristic is attributed to another person relative to oneself is a function of a self-evaluation conflict made up of oppositely directed self-validation tendencies and a tendency to avoid loss of self-esteem.

The interpretation of the data in terms of dissonance reduction alone is not compelling.[1] The removal of self-contradiction, as a drive in itself, does not specifically predict that, under *both* *Negative-* and *Positive-Disclosure* conditions, subjects who experienced strong dissonance would project unfavorable personality characteristics. But this is precisely what did occur. Of course, it cannot be concluded either that the need to avoid loss of self-esteem is the exclusive determinant of projection. Indeed, it can be argued that a greater amount of projection occurred under an experimental condition where the self-esteem threat was relatively weak. Thus, where unfavorable information was disclosed to the individual, one might contend that subjects in whom a negative self-evaluation was initially induced were *more* threatened with a loss of self-esteem than subjects in whom a positive self-evaluation was induced. Yet the latter group of subjects showed a greater amount of projection.

The findings seem to indicate that a superego-id conflict is not a necessary condition for projection. The suggestion that the individual was a latent homosexual, presumably a severe shock to the superego, was constant for all subjects, regardless of the self-evaluations which had been induced in them. Furthermore,

1. We are unable to explain the failure to duplicate Bramel's (1962) finding that subjects who have a positive self-evaluation project more homosexuality.

projection was observed in the complete absence of morally offensive disclosures. For most male subjects, the suggestion that they were extremely virile could not be construed as a threat to their consciences.

Whether the partner was similar or dissimilar to the subject evidently had no effect on the attribution of unfavorable personality characteristics to him. It had earlier been reasoned that projection would be facilitated if the partner was comparable to the subject in some way—that is, if he was part of the subject's judgmental frame of reference. This argument is still intuitively cogent. However, by attributing unfavorable personality characteristics to his partner, the individual tries to differentiate himself from the partner, and, if this is the function of projection, similarity of the partner should operate to inhibit it. Perhaps we should recognize degrees of projection. In a mild form, the individual seeks merely to establish that he is not the only possessor of the trait. By attributing it to others, he does not stand alone. For a mild projection, similarity to others is helpful. In the case of strong projection, not only do others have the negative trait, but they have it in greater quantity. In this case, dissimilarity makes projection easier. So similarity either opposes or facilitates projection, depending upon the strength of the projection tendency. It would seem to be a reasonable conjecture that this tendency in turn depends upon the strength of the self-evaluation conflict, but further research is clearly necessary to specify the role of similarity in projection.

REFERENCES

Bramel, Dana. "A Dissonance Theory Approach to Defensive Projection," *Journal of Abnormal and Social Psychology,* LXIV (1962), 121–129.

11 Self-Validation and Competitive Behavior

The effects of a self-validation need have been interpreted conceptually in terms of the resolution of a self-evaluation conflict. Under conditions that have been specified in the preceding three chapters, the tendency to validate one's worth has been shown to lead to a negative self-evaluation and to the attribution of negative personality characteristics to another person. There is a somewhat different line of approach to the theoretical analysis of self-validation which has implications for interpersonal competitiveness.

There is a large class of situations—for example, the school-room, athletics, teen-age dating, the Army, the academic and business worlds—in which various social and material rewards may be obtained through interpersonal competition, and in some cases, can only be obtained in this manner. It is a matter of common observation that, in such situations, the amount of reward for which the individual competes or the amount of competitiveness he displays in seeking rewards is influenced by his self-evaluation. Several conceptual mechanisms may be identified in this relationship. One obvious one is that by achieving rewards the individual can upgrade his status and thereby enhance his self-esteem. Competitive behavior, in other words, functions to raise the self-evaluation or to avoid a loss of self-evaluation. It probably can be assumed that the strength of this need depends to a large degree on the amount of deprivation the individual feels with respect to himself. Thus, within limits, the less the value the individual places upon himself, the stronger his motivation for certain classes of available rewards upon which the evaluation of himself is contingent. If it is possible to obtain such rewards, stronger self-esteem motivation should lead to greater competitiveness. A familiar example in our rich, mobile society is the compulsive striving observed in some culturally or economically deprived individuals.

The amount of competitiveness displayed by an individual is not only motivated by the need for self-esteem, but is affected by his estimates of success and failure in the particular reward-seeking situation. Self-evaluation is a determinant of such estimates. When the problem of the "underachiever" is discussed, for example, it is this function of self-evaluation which is salient. Thus, "Johnny doesn't compete because he lacks confidence in himself." To the extent that the individual's self-evaluation is based upon or related to the ability required to achieve rewards in the particular situation, one can predict less competitiveness, the lower the self-evaluation.

A third effect of self-evaluation upon competitiveness can occur by way of the self-validation motive. In general, if the individual considers his estimate of himself to be highly valid, his behavior should not belie or contradict that self-evaluation. Assuming the individual perceives that there is a correlation between the amount of reward achieved and one's worth, he should be expected to obtain only that amount of reward which correctly reflects his existing self-evaluation. Such a self-validation tendency should result in a rough proportionality between competitive reward-seeking behavior and the existing self-evaluation. Thus, individuals who have a low evaluation of themselves should tend to compete less than individuals whose self-evaluation is relatively high.

It is clear that the relationship between self-evaluation and competitiveness is a highly complicated one. To draw conclusions about any one of the conceptual processes intervening between these two variables obviously requires experimental arrangements and controls which weaken or rule out alternative interpretations. Accordingly, there are several control possibilities in checking the self-validation interpretation of competitive behavior.

Although an interpretation of competitiveness based on the need for self-esteem forecasts an outcome opposite to that based on the self-validation interpretation, it is necessary to provide some theoretical rationale for this prediction. In the case of the self-esteem need, one fundamental assumption is made. In order for a low self-evaluation to generate a relatively strong drive for self-enhancement, it is assumed that the individual must perceive that he *can* improve his worth in the area on which his self-evaluation is based. Only if there is hope of improvement can low self-evaluation promote greater competitiveness than high self-evaluation. If the individual is led to believe that the personality characteristics which comprise his low self-evaluation are invariant, that is, cannot be changed for the better, a strong self-esteem drive is not likely to be generated. As far as self-validation is concerned, it is probably fair to assume that the need is strengthened under these conditions. Evaluations of unchangeable personality characteristics are considered to be highly valid *because* of their unchangeability.

In order to deal with the argument that the individual who has a relatively low self-evaluation competes less because of his lack of confidence, two controls can be introduced. First, the objective probability of obtaining maximum rewards should be made as high as is practicable. When the risk of getting no reward is negligible, competitiveness cannot easily be said to be determined by confidence: The individual with a low self-evaluation should not estimate that his chances of success are any less than those of the individual with a high self-evaluation. Second, the personality content which the individual is led to evaluate more or less positively can be of such a nature and on such a level of generality as to imply neither the presence nor absence of the specific ability required to compete successfully. Such controls, of course, are not perfect, but they do permit a rational comparison of alternative interpretations of data. A preliminary pair of experiments was conducted to check the prediction that the degree of interpersonal competitiveness shown in the pursuit of rewards depends upon the individual's self-evaluation.

PROCEDURE AND MEASURES

The subjects were female volunteers, recruited from various undergraduate classes. Pairs were scheduled at random for the approximately one-hour session. When the subjects entered the room, the experimenter told them that the psychology department was evaluating a new examination for possible use on incoming freshmen and that all volunteers for psychology experiments were to be given it. The test, subjects were told, was a highly valid measure of how well a person will succeed outside school situations. The essence of the orienting remarks was as follows:

> Although many tests of intellectual capacity now predict how well an individual can do in school, no tests currently in use take account of maturity, creativity, and the ability to handle imaginatively problems that fall outside familiar patterns. This constellation of personality traits contributes to an individual's effectiveness as a person. It is so basic that it has been termed the "X" factor. A reliable measure

of the "X" factor has been discovered to be the individual's power of word discrimination and usage.

Following this statement, the experimenter administered a vocabulary test[1] to each subject privately. The subject was instructed to choose, of four cartoon-like pictures, the one which best illustrated the meaning of a standard word. There were fifteen words in the test. When the two subjects finished, the experimenter scored them one at a time, indicating the subject's grade on a self-evaluation form which she was then asked to fill out. In each experimental pair, one subject was given a score of 38, with an equivalent percentile rank of 60 per cent, and the other was given a score of 45, with an equivalent percentile rank of 97 per cent.

To check on the success of the experimental induction of self-evaluation, the subjects rated themselves on twenty scales, each of which described eight degrees of a personality trait. The list included a variety of test-relevant characteristics like "creativity," "maturity," "efficiency," "leadership," and so on. When the ratings had been completed, the experimenter dissociated himself from the self-evaluation procedure by saying, "Now we can move on to the experiment for which I brought you here." This was done so that the personality characteristics on which the self-evaluations were based would not be perceived as being directly relevant to the kind of skill involved in the experiment proper. The experimenter then described a number of interpersonal relationships, such as bargaining in business, making plans for a sales campaign, discussing military strategy, and so on, which often involve making a choice the outcome of which depends upon a choice made by someone else. The subjects were told they would play a game which would provide social psychology with important information about social interaction. Observing various aspects of social interaction, they were told, was the main object of the experiment. Subjects were then seated at tables on opposite sides of a partition, and each was

1. "The Full-Range Picture Vocabulary Test" of R.B. Ammons and H.S. Ammons.

presented with the following matrix, describing the number of points which could be earned, depending on the combination of choices made by the subject and her partner.

		Player Two	
		red	green
	red	1,1	0,2
Player One			
	green	2,0	0,0

A careful description of the "payoff" possibilities was then privately given each subject being considered Player One:

> As you can see, if you both choose red, you both get one point. If Player One chooses green, and Player Two selects red, the first player gets both points, and the second player gets none. If Player One chooses red and Player Two selects green, Player Two receives both points, and Player One get none. If you both choose green, neither gets any points. There are thus two courses open to you. You may implicitly work out a system of cooperation, or you can go out for points. It depends on how many points you want. The choice is up to you. We don't care which choice you make. After each trial, I will write down the points you earned on that trial. Knowing the points you received and the choice you made, you ought to be able to tell what your partner has chosen. There will be fifty trials.

On each trial, the subjects simultaneously indicated their red or green choices on slips of paper and handed them to the experimenter. After a moment of feigned calculating, each subject was shown the score she had received on that trial. During the game, according to a prearranged schedule, each subject was led to believe that her partner made thirty-one (62 per cent) red, "cooperative" choices. The red and green choices reported to the subject as those made by the partner were distributed throughout the fifty trials without forming a systematic pattern. This distribution was, of course, in a fixed order for all subjects under both conditions of self-evaluation.

For reasons that will become clear as we proceed, a second experiment, with a new sample of female undergraduates, was conducted soon after the first was concluded. Although the same test was used to establish high and low self-evaluation, the procedure which the subjects had to follow differed radically from that of the first experiment. In the second experiment, the subjects were told that the chairman of the psychology department wanted all participants in experiments to take a test of an important nonacademic personality characteristic or ability. Again, the experimenter dissociated himself from the test, but considerable detail about the ability being measured was given in order to impress the subject with the fact that everyone possessed it to some degree and that it was a fixed personality characteristic.

Too many intelligence tests are devoid of requirements for the use of imagination. They present problems which have rather unequivocal answers which the individual either does or does not know. However, most real-life problems are not like that. First of all, they are not clear-cut, but full of ambiguity. Second, a frequent method of attack is to rule out those solutions which are *not* good. This is the essence of creativity—imaginative persistence along a line of thought, setting aside interfering or diametrically opposed meanings and thoughts. To find out how much of this most fundamental characteristic you have, we are going to present you with a number of cards.

On each card there are four drawings of people, objects, or events. The procedure for getting a valid measure of your basic creative potential—called, by the authors of the test, "Inverse Creativity," or simply, "I.C."—is for you to indicate within ten seconds which concept, represented by one of these illustrations, is *furthest removed* in meaning from the meaning of a word which I shall present to you.

When the subject had responded to the fifteen words and corresponding sets of pictures, the experimenter said essentially as follows:

> I now am supposed to give you an appraisal of your performance and tell you more about this fundamental aspect of your personality. Here is your raw score and your percentile rating. (The same as in the first experiment—38 and 60 per cent or 45 and 97 per cent.) I might mention, while you are considering your score, that the test is very reliable and valid. Here is a table of correlations which the test has with other tests. You can see that the correlations are in the nineties. The I.C. test also is a very basic one; the constellation of traits it measures has ramifications in many intellectual spheres. The I.C. is important in one's business and professional career, as well as in home and social situations.
>
> Before we're finished with this test, I am required to get some more data from you. Here is another form which they want you to fill out. It is a self-evaluation form which covers a wide area of your personality. Please rate yourself on the 8-point scale in each of the twenty personality characteristics on the sheet.

Once the subject's evaluation of himself had been checked with exactly the same instrument used in the first study, that is, the twenty scales which measured degrees of positive and negative personality traits, the experimenter put the forms away and turned to the game situation: "We can get on to the main experiment, the one for which I brought you here." The same matrix was used, the same information about scoring was given, and again it was emphasized that the choice of a competitive or cooperative strategy was entirely up to the subject.

THE CREATION OF HIGH AND LOW SELF-EVALUATION

The effectiveness of the experimental inducement of high or low self-evaluation in terms of basic creative potential and personal effectiveness was checked by examining the subject's general personal attractiveness in his own eyes. The ratings of the assorted personality characteristics were scored so that the closer the score was to 1, the higher the subject's rating of himself as a total personality. Table 36 presents the mean ratings under the two experimental conditions of the first and second experiments, separately and combined.[2]

TABLE 36

MEAN RATING OF OWN PERSONALITY BY SUBJECTS UNDER HIGH- AND LOW-SELF-EVALUATION CONDITIONS

	Self-Evaluation		
	High	Low	
First Experiment	63.6*	66.4	
	(N = 17)	(N = 12)	
Second Experiment	54.6	68.4	t = 1.98, p < .05
	(N = 10)	(N = 7)	
Combined	60.1	67.2	

* The lower the number, the higher the self-evaluation.

Although the direction of the differences indicates that the experimental treatment was successful in both experiments, only in the second study can the difference be considered a reliable one. The weak difference in the self-ratings of personality in the first experiment prompted a change to the procedure employed in the second experiment. In the original study, the identification of the picture which best expressed the meaning of the standard word was rather easy for most subjects. Post-experimental interviews suggested that subjects had difficulty in viewing themselves as extremely well endowed in creative potential

2. In the first experiment, it was possible to compute a score representing the subject's actual verbal intelligence as measured by the test. This analysis showed that the average level of intelligence of the subjects assigned to the two experimental conditions was virtually identical.

and personal effectiveness because of success on such a simple test. In the second experiment, the identification of the picture which is the furthest removed in meaning from the standard word seemed to be a more plausible and reliable reflector of basic "Inverse Creativity."

COMPETITIVE CHOICE BEHAVIOR

The data of major interest are the green choices made by each of the two subjects during the experimental session. These may be considered competitive choices in that they could net the subject a maximum number of points and hold the partner's score on the trial to nothing. Since each subject presumably came to notice that his partner had a predilection for red choices—thirty-one out of the fifty trials—his choice of the green alternative was perceived as highly likely to result in a maximum reward. The question is, how much competitive behavior occurs under the experimental conditions of both experiments? Table 37 presents these data.

TABLE 37

MEAN NUMBER OF GREEN (COMPETITIVE) CHOICES BY SUBJECTS
UNDER HIGH- AND LOW-SELF-EVALUATION CONDITIONS

	Self-Evaluation				
	High		*Low*		
	Choices	Points	Choices	Points	
First Experiment	30.5	49.2	26.2	46.1	
	(N = 17)		(N = 12)		
Second Experiment	31.1	50.2	21.3	44.6	t = 3.00,
	(N = 10)		(N = 7)		p < .01*
Combined	30.7		24.5		t = 2.63,
					p < .01*

* Tests of differences between conditions in the number of green choices.

In both studies, more green choices tend to be made by subjects in whom a high self-evaluation was induced. The difference between conditions is statistically reliable in the second study, despite the very small number of cases.

High self-evaluation subjects also earned more points on the average (as indicated by the figures in Table 37). It will be recalled that the number of points earned by subjects over the fifty trials depended generally upon the subject's choices and the experimentally programmed choices thought to have been made by the partner. Since the latter were more often red (62 per cent), the objective opportunity for subjects to receive the maximum payoff on each trial was high. The number of two-point payoffs obtained by the subject specifically depended upon the frequency of green choices he made *and* upon his making them on the trial when the partner had made a red choice. Unless the unlikely assumption is made that ability to anticipate red choices or the strategy of how to play differed between the experimentally induced self-evaluation conditions, subjects who made more green choices should be expected to have earned more points.

In order to determine whether the greater competitiveness on the part of subjects with high self-evaluations was maintained throughout the game, the fifty trials were arbitrarily divided into five blocks of ten trials each. The mean number of green choices made by the subjects in each trial block under the two self-evaluation conditions is given in Table 38.

Without exception, in each portion of the fifty trials examined and in both experiments, subjects with a high self-evaluation make more green choices than their low-self-evalua-

TABLE 38

MEAN NUMBER OF GREEN (COMPETITIVE) CHOICES IN
BLOCKS OF TEN TRIALS

	First Experiment		Second Experiment	
Trials	High	Low	High	Low
1–10 (3) *	5.0	4.3	5.3	4.4
11–20 (4)	5.9	5.3	6.1	4.3
21–30 (4)	5.9	5.3	6.6	3.7
31–40 (5)	6.4	6.0	6.6	4.4
41–50 (3)	7.0	5.3	6.5	4.4

* In parentheses, the number of green choices thought to be made by partner but actually programmed by the experimenter.

tion counterparts. The discrepancies in means between the two self-evaluation conditions are, in most comparisons, about the same size. The few unusually large discrepancies are presumably due to changes in the number of green choices as the game progresses. Thus, in the first study, there is apparently an increasing tendency to make green choices. The difference between the mean of the first trial block and the mean of the last block or, in the case of the *Low-Self-Evaluation* condition, the next to the last block, is statistically reliable. But the subjects in the second study under both self-evaluation conditions show no reliable increase in their green choices. Indeed, the succession of means in the *Low-Self-Evaluation* condition of the second study is remarkably stable, considering the small number of cases.

The evidence in the first study for increased competitiveness from the initial block of ten trials to blocks later in the series can be interpreted in several ways. First, it is possible that the subjects of both self-evaluation conditions tended to increase the level of reward they considered appropriate. This possibility makes sense when it is recalled that, in the first study, the high-and-low-self-evaluation subjects did not differ significantly in the evaluation of their own personalities (see Table 36). Such relative uncertainty as to their self-evaluations could have made for an initial lack of clarity as to what the appropriate level of reward should be. Another possibility is that success in the form of two-point payoffs affected the confidence of subjects or the subjective attractiveness of the rewards being obtained. However, one would have to explain why this did not happen in the second study. Finally, part of the increased competitiveness in the first experiment may simply reflect a cautiousness which characterized the beginning trials of the game. No doubt it took some trials before the subjects figured out that the partner had a predilection for red choices.

ASSESSMENT

The experimental findings leave little doubt that an individual's evaluation of himself affects the level of competitiveness he displays in the kind of interpersonal situation we have investigated. The data support the hypothesis that competition for rewards tends to reflect what subjects consider themselves to be worth generally. To put the thesis differently, competition for rewards tends to be maintained at a level which does not invalidate the individual's self-evaluation. In the light of the data, however, let us reconsider the alternative interpretations that were suggested.

One possible determinant of competitiveness was said to be the need for self-esteem itself. Thus, in order to enhance his status in his own eyes, the individual strives to amass the rewards which are potentially available to him. According to our earlier analysis, however, it is the individual with a low self-evaluation who has the stronger need for self-esteem and, hence, might have been expected to compete more vigorously than the individual with high self-esteem. On the basis of the actual findings, therefore, the self-esteem interpretation of competitiveness cannot be considered a viable alternative to the self-validation one.

A second possible explanation turns out to be a more serious contender. The question was asked: Does self-evaluation have its effect on competitiveness by way of giving the subject more, or less, confidence about achieving success? If it is assumed that subjects in both conditions of self-evaluations correctly perceive the relatively low risk of getting a zero payoff because of the infrequency of green choices by the partner, then differential confidence associated with high and low self-evaluation does not appear to be an especially compelling explanation of the findings. Presumably, for differential confidence to be operative, there needs to be a material risk. It is also not too convincing to argue that the "X" factor and "Inverse Creativity," those vague and general personality characteristics on which the high and low self-evaluations were based, could have been regarded by the subjects as an aid in anticipating the partner's trial-by-trial choices. Nevertheless, despite the arguments to the contrary, the "confidence" interpretation of the difference in competitiveness cannot definitely be ruled out. The objective risk of the partner making a green, zero-payoff choice was *not* zero; over the fifty trials, the probability of this happening was .38. It also needs to be emphasized that what is decisive is not objective, but subjective, probability. Finally, despite our attempts to separate the personality characteristics on which high and low self-evaluations were based from the skills necessary in the game situation, some subjects might have perceived a connection. Altogether then, it is possible that subjects in whom a low self-evaluation was induced had relatively less confidence than high self-evaluation subjects, even in a situation where they could have succeeded with the maximum payoff 62 per cent of the time.

For further clarification, the experiment and its results can be examined from more general frames of reference. Thus, for example, the sequence of trials can be viewed as a situation in which the subject repeatedly sets an aspiration as to the desired amount of reward. According to the level-of-aspiration model, how much reward the individual wants at any given trial, that is, how much he is willing to compete for, depends upon the attractiveness of the reward and the probability of obtaining it. In general, aspiration has been shown to be a function of the actual achievement of the reward to which the individual aspires. Such success theoretically raises the probability of future success and/or the attractiveness of the reward. Concerning the present experiment, one might hold that the differential competitiveness between high- and low-self-evaluation subjects was due to the different amounts of psychological success which these subjects experienced. Thus, for example, the argument might run that high-self-evaluation subjects not only felt more confident about making successful green choices, but subjectively felt more rewarded by the two points they were confident of making than did low-self-evaluation subjects. The difficulty with this view is that successful achievement of aspiration should theoretically lead to regular increases in aspiration and, accordingly, in competitiveness. Since there is at best weak evidence for steadily increasing competitiveness—and this shown only in the first experiment—successful achievement of aspiration would not appear to be a determinant of competitiveness. Therefore, self-evaluation cannot be said to affect competitiveness through such a process.

A question may be raised as to the role of game strategy and similar motivations in the subject's green and red choices. It could be contended that subjects made green choices, not to acquire rewards appropriate to their self-evaluations, but in order to correctly anticipate their partner's choices as often as possible. In other words, subjects literally played a game in trying to figure out their partner's strategy. A similar point of view is reflected in the type of experiment and theory known as probability learning. According to this conceptual framework, the subject's task is to learn to maximize the occasions when his choices coincide with the reinforcement schedule—the choices determined by the experimenter in advance to be rewarding. Although game strategy and probability learning were un-doubtedly involved in the choices made by subjects in the present experiment, such abilities and motivational orientations could not readily account for the difference in frequency of choices obtained between the self-evaluation conditions.

None of these general theoretical approaches seems to pro-vide a satisfactory alternative to the self-validation interpretation concerning the effect of self-evaluation upon competitiveness. To tighten this interpretation, experiments are now being de-signed with the objective of ruling out confidence as the factor through which self-evaluation exerts its effect. In the last analysis, it may be impossible to ascribe competitive choice behavior un-equivocally to the need to maintain a valid self-evaluation as long as there is any risk of loss or lack of reward involved. Accord-ingly, a more clear-cut check on the role of cognitive validation in the making of choices is indicated. One possible approach is to link the individual's self-evaluation directly to his aspiraton—the amount of reward he desires—without having to infer the latter from his competitive choices. If self-evaluation can be shown to affect the choice of reward in a situation where there is no risk involved whatsoever, that is, where the desired reward is guaran-teed, then any differential confidence associated with self-evaluation would be quite irrelevant as an explanation of such reward aspiration. To state the matter positively, if subjects in whom a high self-evaluation has been induced demand a larger reward than subjects in whom a low self-evaluation has been induced, there would be support for the theoretical contention that the amount of reward chosen functions to validate the self-evaluation. A fairly simple experiment was suggested by this line of reasoning.

PROCEDURE AND MEASURES

Individual subjects who were asked to volunteer for an experiment in industrial psychology filled out a so-called Cornell Personality Inventory. The inventory contained forty-five true or false statements about the individual's self or social environment —for example, "I do not worry about catching diseases" or "My mother or father often made me obey even when I thought it unreasonable." Upon completion of the questionnaire, the experimenter scored each item, referring to a well-worn key in full view of the subject. After some five minutes, the subject was asked if he wanted to know the results of the personality test. After the subject's assent (all said yes), he was given a standard test report form on which were arrayed sets of raw scores and percentile equivalents of three subscales ostensibly derived from the inventory. The descriptions of the three subscales which the subjects read were as follows:

Personal Efficiency

PE is essentially an index of the effectiveness of the individual in using his native abilities. Although individuals differ markedly in their endowment of intelligence and various forms of talent, they also differ in how efficiently they use what they have. A high score on the PE scale indicates that the individual is performing as well as his abilities permit, whereas a low score indicates that factors, often emotional in origin, are interfering with his performance.

Social Creativity

> SC is an index of the effectiveness of the individual in relating to others in his social environment. Like the PE scale, it is an efficiency measure, although in the social rather than the cognitive area. A low score indicates social insensitivity and often, but not always, distorted social perception. A high score indicates a healthy and comfortable adjustment to others.

Personal Unity

> UN is a measure of the tendency for the individual to be divided against himself or to be free of such self-defeating conflict. Individuals scoring low on this scale typically exhibit considerable anxiety and doubt over their basic orientation in life, their own personal worth, and their relations with others. High-scoring individuals, on the other hand, are typified by a healthy and realistic self-confidence.

In the *High-Self-Evaluation* condition, scores on all three subscales were at the upper end of the range and thus presented the general picture of a healthy and attractive personality. Subjects in the *Low-Self-Evaluation* condition were given scores at the lower end of the range. In terms of personal efficiency, social creativity, and personal unity, they presumably received the picture of a relatively unhealthy and unattractive personality.

After the subject had finished reading the test report, the experimenter said there would be another brief personality form. The form—actually used to check on the success of the experimental induction—consisted of fifteen 7-point bipolar scales for self-description. The scales were in the format used to establish the "Semantic Differential," involving pairs of highly evaluative adjectives (Osgood, Suci, & Tannenbaum, 1953). When the subjects had finished describing themselves on these scales, the experimenter made the following remarks:

The study for which you volunteered is being done on an outside contract with a major manufacturing corporation. The chairman of the psychology department has given us permission to use the facilities here and to run students as subjects on three conditions. First, we must make it clear to everyone concerned that this is not an official program of either the department or the university. Secondly, all subjects must be paid, and thirdly, we agree to administer the two personality tests which you have just taken so that the department will have some data as to the kinds of people who volunteer for experiments.

Although I am not at liberty to divulge the identity of the firm with which we have the contract, I can tell you that it is one of the world's largest manufacturers of automobiles. And to be perfectly honest with you, the present study is not so much concerned with the theoretical importance of the results as with the practical applications. What we are being paid to do is gather information which will enable our client to reduce its labor costs and, in turn, increase its margin of profit.

You are probably already familiar with many of the technical and economic aspects of automation. These have been thoroughly investigated and the major findings reported in the popular press. However, many psychological aspects of automation remain unknown factors. One problem of particular importance is the relationship between physical discomfort and work output. To put this into experimental terms, the question is how the amount of pain that an individual experiences affects the speed and quality of his work. You will be performing various simple tasks with your dominant hand, and shocks of varying intensities will be delivered at random intervals to your other hand. The intensities will range from very mild up almost to the limit of physiological tolerance.

> Ordinarily, we pay subjects a set amount of money,
> but, because of the unusual nature of this experiment
> and the stress to which you will be subjected, you will
> be allowed to determine your own rate of pay, within
> certain limits, of course.

At this point, the subject was handed a voucher labeled "Work-Interference Study." Listed on the voucher was a sequence of ten payments, ranging from 50¢ to $5.00 in 50¢ intervals. When the voucher was returned, the experimenter said:

> Before we go on, I'd like to tell you about another
> study that I am recruiting for now. This will take
> sixteen hours of your time, from eight one evening
> until noon the following day. You will be allowed
> eight hours sleep and will be served a substantial
> breakfast in the morning. During the four hours in the
> evening and the four hours in the morning, you will
> work on some simple, routine tasks. None of them
> is strenuous. Physiological measures will be taken
> throughout the entire period, while you are awake and
> while you are sleeping. There will be no shocks or
> other unpleasant experiences involved. Assuming that
> you will be able to fit this into your schedule, will you
> fill this out.

The experimenter then handed the subject a second voucher labeled "Fatigue-Recovery Study," this one with a series of ten payments ranging from $2.50 to $25.00 in intervals of $2.50. When this had been filled out, the experimenter told the subjects that they had been in an experiment and that it was all over. He proceeded with a detailed explanation of the experiment's rationale and the purpose of the various instructions. All subjects were paid the same amount for their participation.

EFFECTIVENESS OF THE SELF-EVALUATION INDUCTION

How adequate our procedure was in getting the subject to hold himself in high or low self-esteem can be estimated from the ratings he made on the fifteen evaluative traits. Table 38 shows the mean ratings made by the subjects in the *High-* and *Low-Self-Evaluation* conditions.

TABLE 39

MEAN SELF-RATING BASED ON FIFTEEN PERSONALITY TRAITS
Experimental Condition

High Self-Evaluation	Low Self-Evaluation
(N = 16)	(N = 16)
5.13	4.51

t = 2.87, p < .01

It is evident that the induction procedure was successful. Those in whom a high self-evaluation was induced did indeed tend to rate themselves higher on the assorted personality traits than those in whom a low self-evaluation was induced.

AMOUNT OF REWARD DESIRED

The data of basic interest, of course, are the amounts of remuneration requested in advance for participation in the two kinds of experiments described by the experimenter for the subject's consideration. Table 39 presents the average amount of money asked for by the high- and low-self-evaluation subjects.

TABLE 40

MEAN AMOUNT OF MONEY REQUESTED FOR
PARTICIPATION IN EXPERIMENTS
Type of Experience

Self-Evaluation	Shock	Overnight
High (N = 16)	$3.94	$21.88
Low (N = 16)	$3.94	$18.28

t = 1.91, p < .07

There is no difference whatever between self-evaluation groups in the payment requested for the series of shocks to be experienced. But for the future, overnight stint, it is clear that the high-self-evaluation subjects want more money. On the average, they ask $3.60 more than do the low-self-evaluation subjects.

The immediacy and real danger represented by the shock might have overwhelmed both groups of subjects, making the consideration of reward quite irrelevant. Or both groups, in such perilous circumstances, might have demanded a near-maximum amount. In fact, the amount of money requested by both groups was one scale step below the maximum. The overnight experience was primarily a demand on the individual's time and thus, presumably, requires setting aside other important goals. It is in this context that higher aspiration on the part of high-self-evaluation subjects shows up.

REFERENCES

Osgood, C., Suci, G., and Tannenbaum, P. *The Measurement of Meaning*. Urbana, Ill.: University of Illinois Press, 1957.

12 Recapitulation and Perspective

In this book, we have attempted to work through some of the implications of a basically simple theoretical process which, in one form or another, has been employed in social psychology for well over two decades. The theoretical assumption which has formed the basis of various experimental hypotheses is that, under a wide range of conditions, the individual is motivated to form and maintain subjectively valid evaluations of the self and the social environment. When examined from this point of view, many forms of attraction and hostility can be interpreted, in part, as attempts of the individual to validate his evaluations of himself and other persons. Before discussing the substantive conclusions of the experiments, it would be useful to review some background theory.

221

If it is possible to characterize the prevailing conceptual approach to attraction and hostility, it would be an approach based upon a need-satisfaction–frustration model. According to this model, the attractiveness of another person is a function of the need satisfaction which that person brings about, whereas hostility toward another person is a function of the need frustration which this person imposes. The attractiveness of the self may also be interpreted in terms of a need-satisfaction model. Thus, for example, when the self is a source of frustration, it is disliked. Considering the present state of knowledge, however, such a formulation is entirely too general. In order to be able to predict changes in attraction and hostility in a given situation, one must know *which* needs are operating and *which* behaviors and conditions satisfy or frustrate these needs. Along such specific lines, status and security motives have figured importantly as determinants of attraction and hostility. A standard formulation is this: The greater the reduction in the threat of status loss which another person brings about, the more attractive this person becomes to the individual. Hostility toward another person is similarly based upon how much he threatens the individual with a loss of status and/or security. Substantial experimental data appear to be in support of these theories of attraction and hostility.

However, close examination of this empirical work suggests that status and security motives may not be the only determinants of the acts and attitudes which are assumed to reflect attraction. When other persons act in such a way as to reduce threats to the individual's status or to improve his status, the individual may believe that the worth of these persons along certain dimensions is higher than he had originally estimated. It is possible that the increased liking of such persons is due, not to the need to maintain or achieve status or security, but rather to the tendency of the individual to make his evaluations more valid. On the other hand, when these persons increase the threat to the individual's status or security, their value may be perceived as lower than originally estimated. In general, data on interpersonal attraction and hostility may reflect the individual's *re-evaluations* of other persons in response to his need to maintain valid cognitions of their worth. Similarly, when the valid estimate of his worth along some dimension is perceived to be at a lower or higher level than his previous estimate, one may interpret the individual's change in self-attractiveness in terms of movement toward a more valid evaluation.

Cognitive interpretations of attraction and hostility, as well as of other areas of interpersonal relations, are not new in social psychology. According to several cognitive models, changes in the attractiveness of the self and others are essentially reflections of a drive toward consistency among attitudes toward the self and others. However, cognitive-consistency models, like need-satisfaction models, appear to be too general. Almost always, an inconsistency drive like dissonance is decomposable into more specific motivational forces. Thus, when an individual acts to resolve an inconsistency, it could be that he fears social criticism and wants to avoid being considered irrational and stupid. Or, it could be that inconsistency threatens his grasp on reality. The models that have been proposed do not differentiate between these social and cognitive bases of the reaction to inconsistency.

A more specific cognitive-validation need or similar constructs like the needs for cognitive clarity, stability, reality-testing, and so on have been highly useful in interpreting a large variety of social behaviors. Experiments on opinion conformity, conformity in making judgments about physical stimuli, persistence in the setting of aspiration, formation of competitive coalitions, and affiliation preferences all yield data whch can be interpreted in terms of a cognitive-validation process. Yet the evidence is not altogether unequivocal. For one thing, the experimental conditions which have been used in tests of cognitive hypotheses —such as the discrepancy in opinion between an individual and the majority, the size of the majority, the degree of unstructuredness of the stimulus, or the ability differential between the subject and his partners on a task—do not necessarily generate a validation motive. Specifically, for example, the assumption that opinion discrepancy generates a need for "social reality" which brings about conformity pressure is surely untenable if the individual has already validated his opinion. Furthermore, the size of the discrepancy affects the difficulty of achieving uniformity, as well as the pressure toward uniformity. But the major problem in interpreting these data is the lack of attention to the possibility that status and security motivations could have been present along with the validation motive. Testing the hypothesis that a cognitive-validation motive underlies social and self-evaluation requires that the validity of evaluations be manipulated and that status, security, or self-esteem motives be eliminated or held constant. This was the methodological strategy of the research program described in the foregoing chapters. When applied to the domain of attraction and hostility, validation hypotheses have the following general form: If the individual is confronted with reliable evidence that his evaluation of another person or himself is invalid, he tends to change the evaluation in the direction of greater validity. Equivalently, if there is a discrepancy between two or more estimates of his own or another's worth along some dimension, the individual tends to reject the more invalid estimates and to accept the more valid ones. Along the lines of the latter formulation, the validation motive should be aroused when there is a discrepancy between another person's expressed self-evaluation and his true worth, as inferred by various situational and behavioral criteria. In real life, this occurs when the individual interacts with a boastful person, that is, a person whose estimate of his own worth exceeds a valid estimate. As a reflection of the theoretical validation tendency, the individual may be expected to develop a negative attitude toward the boastful person. Evidence of a negative attitude toward an experimentally created boastful person was, in fact, found under conditions where it was highly unlikely that such boastful behavior constituted a status or security threat to the individual. But to some extent, at least, the negative reaction to boastfulness may have been due to the dislike of this form of behavior as such. Among the college-student population, boastfulness is not in good taste. To rule out this alternative explanation, an experiment was designed in which boastfulness was held constant, while the apparently objective status of the boastful person in the area of the boast—presumably reflecting his true worth in that area—was varied. In this situation, the dislike of the boaster was found to decline as the discrepancy between the estimate of the person's true worth and his egregious self-evaluation decreased. Further experiments demonstrated that the effect was not due exclusively to a positive attitude toward the boaster's high status position as such. Direct evidence was also presented that the negative attitude toward a boaster is closely associated with the degree to which his self-defined superiority is considered to be unwarranted.

If the individual reacts negatively to a person's self-evaluation when it is higher than justified according to apparently objective criteria, he should be expected to react positively to a self-evaluation which is lower than it should be. The hypothesized validation motive, in other words, should operate in either direction when the valid estimate of another's worth differs from other estimates, such as his own self-evaluation. Experimental findings confirm this implication: A person who underestimates his abilities tends to be liked more than the person whose low self-evaluation is in line with his apparent objective status.

Of course, positive attitudes toward status and negative attitudes toward boastfulness and self-depreciation exist apart from attitudes which reflect the rejection of invalid evaluation estimates. Although such confounding attitudes toward status and boastfulness were ruled out as the exclusive determinants of attraction, there was still the possibility that each contributed partly. That is, the subject's negative attitude toward a low-status boaster could have consisted of two independent effects: an attitude toward boastfulness and an attitude toward status, rather than a single effect reflecting a cognitive-validation tendency. It was reasoned that this possibility could be ruled out if neither a person's expressed self-evaluation nor his status was employed as an estimate of his worth. Accordingly, a design was set up in which an estimate of the valuation of a person was given by a third party who was unbiased, negatively biased or positively biased. In these bias conditions, the stage is presumably set for the operation of the hypothesized validation tendency: There is a discrepancy between the estimate of the person's worth overtly provided by the informant and the true estimate inferred by taking account of the informant's bias. The experimental data confirmed the deductions: A person who is evaluated negatively by an informant is more disliked when the informant is unbiased than when he is perceived to have a negative bias. Similarly, a person who is evaluated positively by an informant is liked more when the informant is objective than when he is perceived to have a positive bias. Further, an attitude toward a person, based on a negative or positive evaluation of him by an informant, will *change* if the informant is discovered to be biased. The attitude toward the person becomes less negative if the informant is negatively biased and less positive if the informant is positively biased.

The individual's evaluation of himself depends upon the achievement of important goals and upon his adherence to internalized values or norms prescribed by the society in which he lives. This reasonably safe assumption means that, when the individual fails to achieve goals or violates one or more of these norms, the estimate he has of his own worth is lowered. If the individual harbors a validation need with respect to his own evaluation, a norm violation should produce a tendency toward lowered self-attractiveness, reflecting the movement of his self-evaluation downward toward a more valid level. But such a self-devaluation tendency can also be assumed to threaten the individual's self-esteem. And when the latter motive is operating, one can suppose a conflicting tendency to maintain the self-evaluation. Thus, self-attractiveness depends upon the direction in which a self-evaluation conflict is resolved. If the individual can deny that he has violated any norms, the self-devaluation tendency can be eliminated, and he can maintain his self-esteem. The occurrence of such a self-defense is generally based upon the resources and opportunities which are available to the individual. If the individual is permitted to evaluate only himself and cannot blame someone else for his norm-violation, he tends to show the self-devaluation tendency. On the other hand, the existence of expert or authoritative opinion which may be construed as condoning the norm-violating conduct is a common source of self-defense. Several deductions can be made within this framework. Given the same severity of violation, the presence of authoritative opinion supportive of the norm violation should make for more defensive, self-justifying attitudes. Individuals who defend themselves in this way should, as a result, show less negative self-evaluations than those who are not able to deny the norm violation. In the absence of a defensive opportunity, the more severe the norm violation, the greater the tendency toward a downward correction of the self-evaluation to a more valid level. Individuals who show this self-correcting tendency should show, consequently, less self-regard than those who justify their conduct. The attraction of the self thus depends, in general, upon outcome of a self-evaluation conflict, which in turn depends upon the availability of social support for the individual's conduct. Experimental data confirm these deductions.

Projection of unacceptable personality characteristics is another form of defense against corrective self-devaluation tendencies. By attributing to another person or persons as much or more of a negative trait than he himself possesses, the individual is relatively less unattractive to himself. Projection, like the adoption of self-justifying attitudes, can be viewed as an outcome of a self-evaluation conflict of the following sort: An individual who has a relatively positive self-evaluation receives reliable information to the effect that he possesses an extremely negative personality characteristic. Assuming that the area of the personality originally valued positively and the area covered by the unflattering information overlap to some degree, it may be supposed that the individual is in conflict as to which of the two self-evaluations is the more valid. In addition to this purely cognitive conflict, the negative characteristic disclosed to the individual constitutes a threat to his self-esteem. By projecting the negative characteristic onto another person, the individual can satisfy both components of the self-evaluation conflict. Projection of the negative characteristic not only affirms the validity of his existing, positive personality evaluation, but enables the individual to maintain his self-esteem as well.

Self-attractiveness, it can be said, is determined by the projection of negative characteristics, and the amount of projection depends upon the strength of the self-evaluation conflict. In line with this analysis, a greater amount of projection of negative personality characteristics was found to be made by individuals who had a high opinion of themselves and who then received unfavorable information than by those whose existing self-evaluation was negative and who received the same unfavorable information about themselves. The resolution of a self-evaluation conflict through projection theoretically should also occur when the individual's existing self-evaluation is negative and he receives positive information about himself. As before, there is a conflict as to which self-evaluation is valid. Additionally, coinciding with his negative self-evaluation is a persisting tendency to achieve a higher level of self-esteem. By projecting onto others negative personality traits, the individual can resolve the double self-evaluation conflict and thereby become relatively less unattractive to himself. A larger amount of projection did, in fact, tend to occur in the case of a strong self-evaluation conflict than in the case where an individual with an existing positive self-evaluation received information which favorably reflected on his personality. More specifically, the effect of a self-evaluation conflict on projection was represented by reliable statistical interactions of the following form: Subjects with a high self-evaluation who receive unfavorable information about themselves project more than those with a low self-evaluation; subjects with a low self-evaluation who receive favorable information about themselves project more than those with a high self-evaluation.

The hypothesized validation tendency with respect to self-evaluation can be assumed to affect the individual's interpersonal actions and choices, as well as his attitudes and judgments. In line with this general supposition, it was postulated that the individual with a high self-evaluation tends to seek rewards in an amount commensurate with his self-evaluation. The cognitive basis for such a relation between self-evaluation and rewards sought is that rewards which are incommensurate with the self-evaluation would threaten the validity of the evaluation. An implication of this assertion would seem to be that, in a two-person game situation where players can obtain rewards through competition, the individual who has a high self-evaluation will tend to be more competitive and seek higher rewards than the individual with a low self-evaluation. The results of our experiment support this theoretical analysis, although we cannot be absolutely certain that differential confidence which might have been associated with self-evaluation was without effect in determining the subjects' competitive choices. Indeed, it may well be the case that the hypothesized self-validation tendency cannot receive a conclusive test when there is any competitive risk involved in the making of choices. However, it was possible to test the hypothesis in a situation where the individual's choice of reward was direct—that is, not reflected by his competitiveness—and altogether riskless. Thus, subjects in whom a high or low self-evaluation was experimentally induced were asked to state how much money they wished to be paid for participating in two kinds of experiments. For "working" in one of these studies, it was clear that high-self-evaluation subjects made considerably higher "wage demands" than low-self-evaluation subjects. It is reasonable to conclude that aspiration for reward, in a situation where the delivery of the reward is essentially guaranteed and, hence, where differential self-confidence is irrelevant, tends to be commensurate with what the individual believes to be his valuation as a person.

We have taken a step toward isolating and working with some of the dynamics that underlie attraction and hostility. The step has been a small one, and much tracking still needs to be done. A sound plan for future research in the area would seem to be this: more detailed and more refined experimental analyses of the interaction between validation pressures, on the one hand, and self-esteem, social-status, and security motives, on the other.

Subject
Index

231

Name Index

Ammons, H., 204
Ammons, R., 204
Apicella, F., 20, 26
Aronson, E., 44, 48, 49
Arsenian, J., 14, 25
Asch, S., 52, 53, 68
Ax, A., 20, 25

B

Berkowitz, L., 10, 11, 25
Bramel, D., 185, 186, 198
Brehm, J., 47, 49

C

Cartwright, D., 6, 25
Cohen, A., 47, 49
Coules, J., 11, 27

D

Deutsch, M., 16, 25, 32, 49, 53, 68
Dollard, J., 8, 25
Doob, L., 8, 25
Dreyer, A., 57, 68

237